Betty Crocker

small
bites

100 Recipes for the Way You Really Cook

WILEY

Wiley Publishing, Inc.

Copyright © 2011 by General Mills, Minneapolis, Minnesota. All rights reserved.

Published by Wiley Publishing, Inc., Hoboken, New Jersey

Published simultaneously in Canada

For general information on our other products and services or for technical support, please contact our Customer Care Department within the United States at (800) 762-2974, outside the United States at (317) 572-3993 or fax (317) 572-4002.

Wiley also publishes its books in a variety of electronic formats. Some content that appears in print may not be available in electronic books. For more information about Wiley products, visit our web site at www.wiley.com.

Library of Congress Cataloging-in-Publication Data:
Crocker, Betty.
  Betty Crocker small bites : 100 recipes for the way you really cook.
    p. cm.
  Includes index.
  ISBN 978-1-118-12183-2 (cloth/spiral-bound : alk. paper)
  1. Appetizers. I. Title. II. Title: Small bites.
  TX740.C683 2008
  641.8'12—dc22
                        2008009430

General Mills Betty Crocker Kitchens:

Publisher, Cookbooks:
Maggie Gilbert/Lynn Vettel

Manager and Editor, Cookbooks:
Lois Tlusty

Food Editor:
Andi Bidwell

Recipe Development and Testing:
Betty Crocker Kitchens

Photography: General Mills Photography Studios and Image Library

Printed in China
10 9 8 7 6 5 4 3 2 1

Cover photo: Pesto-Cheese Cups
(page 96)

Wiley Publishing, Inc.:

Publisher: Natalie Chapman

Executive Editor: Anne Ficklen

Editor: Adam Kowit

Production Manager: Michael Olivo

Cover Design: Suzanne Sunwoo

Art Director: Tai Blanche

Layout: Indianapolis Composition Services

Manufacturing Manager: Kevin Watt

Our Betty Crocker Kitchens seal guarantees success in your kitchen. Every recipe has been tested in America's Most Trusted Kitchens™ to meet our high standards of reliability, easy preparation and great taste.

Find more great ideas at *BettyCrocker.com*

Dear Friends,

In the mood for food and company but not for a full meal or a formal sit-down affair? Or maybe it's a low-key Saturday at home with the family, and everyone wants just a little of this, a little of that.

Let small bites save the day. Perfect for parties of two, ten, twenty or more, the best thing about them is that no one has to choose just one—not even the cook! And many can be made ahead of time, or have do-ahead components, so you can be sure to enjoy the party along with the rest of your guests.

Everyone will enjoy picking from platters of delectable small bites. One or two Tomato-Basil Bruschetta, a couple of Baked Coconut Shrimp, a few Festive Mini-Tacos— and there's still room for more!

Even dessert doesn't have to be "just one." Take a Tiny Lemon Gem Tart; pick a Peppermint Shortbread Bite; slip a slice of apple into the Caramel-Coffee Fondue.

So set out the small bites and start the party!

Enjoy,
Betty Crocker

contents

Enjoy the Variety

The beauty of small bites is in their versatility. You can make one kind for a snack, a few kinds and make a meal of them or go all out with a big variety for a cocktail party. Whatever the occasion, you'll be able to satisfy a variety of tastes.

Small Bites, Big Group—Let's Party!

Entertaining with small bites can be easy! Follow these guidelines for stress-free party planning.

THE PARTY PLAN

- Create your menu with an eye towards the types of foods, flavors and textures.

- Map out a timeline. When is the party? How much time do you have—or need—to prepare the food?

- Make-ahead makes it easy! Ask yourself what work can be done in advance so you're not scrambling at the last minute. Chapter 3 is filled with do-ahead recipes, and many recipes can be made weeks ahead and frozen or have make-ahead components with minor last-minute prep.

CHOOSING RECIPES

- Mix hot appetizers and cold appetizers. Having a combination will be easier for you to manage (since cold dishes are usually made ahead), and it gives your guests more variety.

- Select an appetizer or two from different food groups to provide a balanced menu—unless you're serving a dessert buffet!

- Choose recipes that offer a variety of textures and colors. Use colorful serving dishes and paper goods when serving less colorful foods.

- Health-conscious guests may steer clear of the cheesy appetizers, so offer one or two healthful appetizers and a selection of non-alcoholic beverages, as well.

SETTING UP FOR THE PARTY

- Set up the small bites spread where it's most convenient—on the dining room table, a picnic table, two card tables placed together, a kitchen counter or desk. Or set up "stations" at smaller tables. Easy access and good flow will eliminate traffic jams!

- Set up self-service coffee and beverage areas or tables. If you're outdoors, fill coolers with beverages and label what's in each.

- Make colorful labels for each food. For unusual foods or ones that contain nuts, include the ingredients on the cards. This way you won't spend all night answering questions!

- Strawberries, raspberries, thin slices of lemon or lime and lemon leaves all make super-easy garnishes for just about any platter. For a dash of elegance, dust desserts with powdered sugar or cocoa.

- Pretend you're a guest and walk through your setup. You'll quickly find out what adjustments you need to make.

SERVING HOT BITES HOT AND COLD BITES COLD

- Hot foods, such as appetizers or finger foods, can be kept hot in a chafing dish. You can also keep extras warm in the oven on the warm setting. Hot dips and spreads can be kept warm in a slow cooker on the low setting or in a fondue pot.

- Store cold foods in the refrigerator until serving time, and set out more as they are needed. When serving foods that need to stay chilled, set their serving bowl or plate in a bowl filled with ice.

- Hot beverages can be made ahead of time and poured into thermal carafes. They stay piping hot, and guests can serve themselves.

How many small bites do you need?

If you're serving them just prior to a meal, allow 4 or 5 hors d'oeuvres per person. If a meal will be served later, 5 or 6 per guest should be fine. If your small bites are the meal, allow 10 to 12 per person.

Menu Starter Set

You can mix and match small bites to create menus for all kinds of occasions and tastes, and here are a few ideas to get you started. But food types, flavors and textures may not be your only considerations. Today's hectic schedules and health consciousness also come into play.

If you're short on time, all recipes in the Superfast Snacks chapter can be prepared in 15 minutes or less. Need make-ahead recipes? The Lazy Day Buffet recipes are doable at least 24 hours ahead of time so all you have to do is serve and eat on the day. If fat content is a consideration, Light Bites have 1g or less of total fat per serving.

CALLING ALL SPORTS FANS (SERVES 8–10)

Spicy Chicken Wings, page 40
Barbecued Pork Crostini, page 124
Beef and Provolone Pinwheels, page 12
Festive Mini-Tacos, page 24
Potato Bites, page 70
Luscious Lemon Squares, page 142

AFTERNOON ON THE DECK (SERVES 10–12)

Endive with Sun-Dried Tomato Chicken Salad, page 16
Crab Cakes with Cilantro Salsa, page 112
Garden Phyllo Quiches, page 97
Roasted Pepper–Tomato Crostini, page 67
Quick Cuke Canapés, page 30
Blue Cheese and Pear Triangles, page 27
White Chocolate–Dipped Strawberries, page 149

WINTERTIME MOVIE NIGHT (SERVES 12–14)

Bacon-Turkey Bites, page 36
Slow Cooker Cranberry Barbecue Meatballs, page 111
Antipasto Pizzettes, page 45
Sweet Potato Fries with Easy Fruit Salsa, page 71
Stuffed Baby Portabella Mushrooms, page 50
Winter Fruit Kabobs with Peach Glaze, page 126
Mini Almond Cheesecakes, page 152
Mini Peanut Butter Cheesecakes, page 153

CASUAL COCKTAIL PARTY (SERVES 20–22)

Beef and Provolone Pinwheels

Pesto Pepperoni Roll-Ups

Cheesy Herb and Turkey Bites

Endive with Sun-Dried Tomato Chicken Salad

Mediterranean Chicken Quesadillas

Corn and Crab Quesadillas

Shrimp with Bourbon Cocktail Sauce

Salmon-Pimiento Appetizers

Festive Mini-Tacos

Sun-Dried Tomato and Prosciutto Pizza

Tomato-Basil Bruschetta

Blue Cheese and Pear Triangles

Double Cheese Bruschetta

Quick Cuke Canapés

Savory Pecans

Italian Sautéed Olives

1

superfast snacks

Ready in 15 minutes or less!

Beef and Provolone Pinwheels

Prep Time: 10 min ▪ Start to Finish: 10 min ▪ 24 Pinwheels

¼ cup mayonnaise or salad dressing
2 cloves garlic, finely chopped
2 flour tortillas (8 inch; from 11.5-oz package)
1 cup fresh spinach
¼ lb thinly sliced deli roast beef
6 slices (¾ oz each) provolone cheese
1 medium tomato, thinly sliced
24 toothpicks

1 In small bowl, mix mayonnaise and garlic. Spread mixture evenly over tortillas.

2 Top tortillas with layers of spinach, beef, cheese and tomato; roll up tightly. Cut each tortilla into 12 pieces; secure with toothpicks. Serve immediately, or refrigerate until serving.

1 Pinwheel: Calories 55 (Calories from Fat 35); Total Fat 4g (Saturated Fat 2g); Cholesterol 10mg; Sodium 85mg; Total Carbohydrate 2g (Dietary Fiber 0g); Protein 3g

Do Ahead: Wrap each uncut roll tightly in plastic wrap and refrigerate up to 24 hours.

Pesto Pepperoni Roll-Ups

Prep Time: 15 min ■ Start to Finish: 15 min ■ 48 Appetizers

½ cup basil pesto
4 pesto-flavor flour tortillas (8 to 10 inch)
1 package (3¼ oz) sliced pepperoni
2 plum (Roma) tomatoes, seeded and chopped
¼ cup chopped yellow or orange bell pepper
¼ cup chopped ripe olives, drained
½ cup shredded mozzarella cheese (2 oz)

1 Spread 2 tablespoons pesto evenly over each tortilla. Arrange 12 pepperoni slices on pesto. Sprinkle tomatoes, bell pepper, olives and cheese evenly over pepperoni to within ½ inch of edges of tortillas.

2 Roll up tortillas tightly. Cut each roll into 8 slices.

1 Appetizer: Calories 40 (Calories from Fat 25); Total Fat 3g (Saturated Fat 1g); Cholesterol 5mg; Sodium 80mg; Total Carbohydrate 2g (Dietary Fiber 0g); Protein 1g

Do Ahead: Wrap each uncut roll tightly in plastic wrap and refrigerate up to 24 hours.

Cheesy Herb and Turkey Bites

Prep Time: 15 min   Start to Finish: 15 min   40 Appetizers

10 thin slices (about 4 inches in diameter) cooked turkey (from 6-oz package)
1/4 cup herb-and-garlic spreadable cheese
1/4 cup finely chopped red bell pepper
40 bite-size garlic-flavored or plain bagel chips or round buttery crackers
Chopped fresh parsley or chives, if desired

1 Unfold each turkey slice and lay flat on work surface. Spread each slice with 1 teaspoon cheese and top with 1 teaspoon bell pepper. Carefully roll up. Cut each roll into 4 pieces.

2 Place each turkey roll on bagel chip. Garnish with parsley. Serve immediately.

1 Appetizer: Calories 20 (Calories from Fat 10); Total Fat 1g (Saturated Fat 0g); Cholesterol 20mg; Sodium 35mg; Total Carbohydrate 1g (Dietary Fiber 0g); Protein 1g

Do Ahead: Follow step 1 and carefully roll up each turkey slice, but do not cut. Cover and refrigerate rolls up to 8 hours. Cut each into 4 pieces and continue as directed.

Endive with Sun-Dried Tomato Chicken Salad

Prep Time: 15 min ▪ Start to Finish: 15 min ▪ 16 Appetizers

½ pint deli chicken salad (1 cup)
¼ cup sliced oil-packed sun-dried tomatoes, drained
2 heads green or red Belgian endive (16 leaves)
¼ cup chopped ripe olives
Chopped fresh parsley

1 In medium bowl, mix chicken salad and tomatoes. Spoon about 1 tablespoon chicken mixture on center of each endive leaf.

2 Top with olives; sprinkle with parsley. Serve immediately.

1 Appetizer: Calories 25 (Calories from Fat 20); Total Fat 2g (Saturated Fat 0g); Cholesterol 5mg; Sodium 50mg; Total Carbohydrate 1g (Dietary Fiber 1g); Protein 2g

If Belgian endive is not available, spoon chicken mixture onto red or yellow bell pepper wedges or cucumbers, halved lengthwise, seeded and cut into thirds.

Mediterranean Chicken Quesadillas

Prep Time: 10 min   Start to Finish: 15 min   16 Appetizers

½ lb cooked chicken or turkey (from the deli) (about 1 cup cut up)
3 plum (Roma) tomatoes
4 flour tortillas (8 to 10 inch)
¼ cup soft cream cheese with roasted garlic (from 8-oz container)
1 cup shredded mozzarella cheese (4 oz)
½ cup crumbled feta cheese (2 oz)
Chopped fresh cilantro or parsley, if desired
Sliced ripe olives, if desired
Sliced jalapeño chile, if desired
Salsa, if desired

1 Heat oven to 450°F. Cut chicken into ½-inch pieces. Chop tomatoes.

2 On ungreased cookie sheet, place 2 tortillas. Spread about 2 tablespoons cream cheese over each tortilla. Top with the chicken, tomatoes, mozzarella cheese and feta cheese. Top with the 2 remaining tortillas.

3 Bake about 5 minutes or just until the cheese is melted.

4 To serve, cut each quesadilla into 8 wedges. Sprinkle with cilantro. Garnish each wedge with an olive or jalapeño chile slice, using a toothpick to hold the olive or chile in place. Serve with salsa.

1 Appetizer: Calories 95 (Calories from Fat 45); Total Fat 5g (Saturated Fat 2g); Cholesterol 20mg; Sodium 160mg; Total Carbohydrate 7g (Dietary Fiber 0g); Protein 6g

If you prefer to buy cooked chicken pieces or cook your own chicken, you'll need 2 or 3 chicken breast halves.

Corn and Crab Quesadillas

Prep Time: 5 min ▪ Start to Finish: 15 min ▪ 18 Wedges

1 package (8 oz) cream cheese, softened
1 can (11 oz) whole kernel corn, drained
½ cup chopped fresh cilantro or parsley
5 medium green onions, chopped (⅓ cup)
1 jar (2 oz) diced pimientos, drained
½ teaspoon black pepper
¼ teaspoon ground red pepper (cayenne)
1 lb chopped cooked crabmeat or imitation crabmeat (2 cups)
6 sun-dried tomato or spinach-cilantro flavored flour tortillas (8 to 10 inch)
1 tablespoon butter or margarine, melted

1 In medium bowl, mix cream cheese, corn, cilantro, onions, pimientos, black pepper and red pepper. Fold in crabmeat. Spread ⅔ cup of the crabmeat mixture over each tortilla; fold tortilla in half, pressing lightly. Brush butter over both sides of each tortilla.

2 In 12-inch skillet, cook 3 tortillas at a time over medium-high heat about 5 minutes, turning once, until light brown. Cut each quesadilla into 3 wedges.

1 Wedge: Calories 140 (Calories from Fat 65); Total Fat 7g (Saturated Fat 4g); Cholesterol 40mg; Sodium 220mg; Total Carbohydrate 12g (Dietary Fiber 1g); Protein 8g

Instead of pimientos, you can substitute roasted red bell peppers, available in jars, drained and chopped, or chopped fresh red bell pepper.

Shrimp with Bourbon Cocktail Sauce

Prep Time: 15 min ▪ Start to Finish: 15 min ▪ About 24 Servings

½ cup mayonnaise or salad dressing
¼ cup cocktail sauce
¼ cup whipping cream
1 tablespoon bourbon, if desired
⅛ teaspoon red pepper sauce
1 lb cooked peeled deveined large shrimp (about 24 to 30), thawed if frozen

1 In small bowl, mix all ingredients except shrimp.

2 Serve sauce as dip for shrimp.

1 Serving: Calories 65 (Calories from Fat 45); Total Fat 5g (Saturated Fat 1g); Cholesterol 40mg; Sodium 100mg; Total Carbohydrate 1g (Dietary Fiber 0g); Protein 4g

For easy eating, pierce the shrimp with frilly toothpicks, or make toothpicks available to those who want them.

Salmon-Pimiento Appetizers

Prep Time: 15 min ▪ Start to Finish: 15 min ▪ 16 Appetizers

1 package (4.5 oz) smoked salmon (hot-smoked), skin removed, flaked
⅓ cup pimiento cheese spread (from 5-oz jar)
2 teaspoons mayonnaise or salad dressing
2 medium green onions, thinly sliced (2 tablespoons)
⅛ teaspoon pepper
16 slices cocktail pumpernickel bread
16 thin slices seedless cucumber
2 tablespoons tiny dill weed sprigs

1 In medium bowl, mix salmon, cheese spread, mayonnaise, onions and pepper. Spread evenly on bread slices.

2 Cut cucumber slices in half almost to edge and twist; place on salmon mixture. Garnish with dill weed sprigs.

1 Appetizer: Calories 45 (Calories from Fat 20); Total Fat 2g (Saturated Fat 1g); Cholesterol 5mg; Sodium 150mg; Total Carbohydrate 4g (Dietary Fiber 0g); Protein 3g

Can't find smoked salmon? Use a 6-ounce can of boneless skinless salmon, drained, instead.

Festive Mini-Tacos

Prep Time: 15 min ▪ Start to Finish: 15 min ▪ 24 Mini-Tacos

¼ cup mayonnaise or salad dressing
½ teaspoon ground cumin
¼ teaspoon salt
⅛ teaspoon ground cinnamon
1 teaspoon honey
1 can (15 oz) black beans, rinsed, drained
⅓ cup thinly sliced celery
1 package (3.8 oz) miniature taco shells (24 shells)
⅓ cup dried cranberries
2 tablespoons chopped fresh cilantro

1 In medium bowl, mix mayonnaise, cumin, salt, cinnamon and honey. Stir in beans and celery.

2 Spoon about 1½ tablespoonfuls mixture into each taco shell. Sprinkle with cranberries and cilantro.

1 Mini-Taco: Calories 65 (Calories from Fat 25); Total Fat 3g (Saturated Fat 0g); Cholesterol 0mg; Sodium 125mg; Total Carbohydrate 10g (Dietary Fiber 2g); Protein 2g

Do Ahead: You can prepare the taco filling 3 to 4 hours ahead of time, and refrigerate. Chop the cilantro and refrigerate. Ask a family member, or a guest who has arrived early, to help fill the mini-shells at the last minute.

Sun-Dried Tomato and Prosciutto Pizza

Prep Time: 5 min ▪ Start to Finish: 15 min ▪ 16 Servings

1 package (10 oz) prebaked thin Italian pizza crust (12 inch)
¼ cup sun-dried tomato spread
3 oz thinly sliced prosciutto, cut into thin strips
2 tablespoons shredded fresh basil leaves
1 cup finely shredded mozzarella cheese (4 oz)

1 Heat oven to 450°F. On ungreased cookie sheet, place pizza crust. Spread with tomato spread. Top with prosciutto, basil and cheese.

2 Bake about 8 minutes or until cheese is melted. Cut into small squares or wedges.

1 Serving: Calories 90 (Calories from Fat 35); Total Fat 4g (Saturated Fat 2g); Cholesterol 10mg; Sodium 220mg; Total Carbohydrate 10g (Dietary Fiber 0g); Protein 5g

Do Ahead: Assemble the pizza up to 2 hours ahead of time. Keep it covered in the refrigerator, and bake just before serving.

Tomato-Basil Bruschetta

Prep Time: 5 min ▪ Start to Finish: 15 min ▪ About 30 Appetizers

2 large tomatoes
2 cloves garlic
¼ cup chopped fresh basil leaves
¼ cup shredded Parmesan cheese
2 tablespoons olive or vegetable oil
½ teaspoon salt
½ teaspoon pepper
1 baguette, 14 to 16 inches long

1 Heat oven to 450°F. Chop tomatoes. Peel and finely chop garlic.

2 In medium bowl, mix tomatoes, garlic, basil, cheese, oil, salt and pepper.

3 Cut baguette into ½-inch slices. On ungreased cookie sheet, place slices. Spoon tomato mixture onto bread.

4 Bake 6 to 8 minutes or until edges of bread are golden brown. Serve warm.

1 Appetizer: Calories 25 (Calories from Fat 10); Total Fat 1g (Saturated Fat 0g); Cholesterol 0mg; Sodium 75mg; Total Carbohydrate 3g (Dietary Fiber 0g); Protein 1g

Roasted Red Pepper Bruschetta: Substitute 2 jars (7 ounces each) roasted red bell peppers, drained, for the tomatoes and ¼ cup chopped fresh parsley for the basil. Sprinkle with 2 tablespoons capers if desired.

To keep appetizers warm longer, heat ovenproof serving plates on the lowest oven setting 5 to 10 minutes before serving. Or, just before using, warm plate by rinsing in hot water; dry with kitchen towel.

Blue Cheese and Pear Triangles

Prep Time: 10 min   Start to Finish: 15 min   24 Triangles

12 slices pumpernickel cocktail bread, cut diagonally into 2 triangles
3 tablespoons mayonnaise or salad dressing
1 medium unpeeled red or green pear, thinly sliced and slices cut in half
2 tablespoons chopped drained roasted red bell peppers (from 7-oz jar)
⅓ cup crumbled blue cheese
⅓ cup chopped walnuts
Fresh marjoram leaves or chopped fresh chives

1 Heat oven to 400°F. On ungreased cookie sheet, place bread. Bake 4 to 5 minutes or until lightly toasted.

2 Spread mayonnaise over bread. Top with pear slices, bell pepper pieces, cheese, walnuts and marjoram. Serve immediately.

1 Triangle: Calories 45 (Calories from Fat 25); Total Fat 3g (Saturated Fat 1g); Cholesterol 5mg; Sodium 60mg; Total Carbohydrate 4g (Dietary Fiber 1g); Protein 1g

Do Ahead: Toast the bread up to 24 hours ahead; store covered at room temperature.

Double Cheese Bruschetta

Prep Time: 15 min ■ Start to Finish: 15 min ■ 18 Appetizers

2 oz feta cheese, crumbled (½ cup)
1 package (3 oz) cream cheese, softened
18 toasted baguette slices, about ¼ inch thick
18 marinated kalamata or Greek olives, pitted and sliced
9 cherry tomatoes, sliced

1 In small bowl, mix feta cheese and cream cheese; spread on baguette slices.

2 Top with olives and tomatoes.

1 Appetizer: Calories 55 (Calories from Fat 25); Total Fat 3g (Saturated Fat 2g); Cholesterol 10mg; Sodium 130mg; Total Carbohydrate 5g (Dietary Fiber 0g); Protein 2g

Sun-Dried Tomato Bruschetta: Spread cream cheese on toasted bread. Top with julienne strips of sun-dried tomatoes packed in oil and herbs, drained. Sprinkle with toasted pine nuts.

Mascarpone Bruschetta: Spread mascarpone cheese on toasted bread. Top with dried cranberries, crumbled dried rosemary leaves and a dash of ground cardamom.

Quick Cuke Canapés

Prep Time: 15 min ▪ Start to Finish: 15 min ▪ 24 Appetizers

2 oz salmon lox, finely chopped
4 oz (half 8-oz package) cream cheese, softened
3/4 teaspoon chopped fresh or 1/4 teaspoon dried dill weed
2 large cucumbers, cut into 1/4-inch slices (24 slices)
Dill weed sprigs, if desired

1 Mix lox, cream cheese and dill weed.

2 Spoon lox mixture onto each cucumber slice. Garnish with dill weed sprigs.

1 Appetizer: Calories 25 (Calories from Fat 20); Total Fat 2g (Saturated Fat 1g); Cholesterol 5mg; Sodium 15mg; Total Carbohydrate 1g (Dietary Fiber 0g); Protein 1g

Add some flare! Place lox mixture in decorating bag fitted with large star tip; pipe 1 heaping teaspoonful onto each cucumber slice. Garnish these quick veggie canapés with cooked shrimp.

Savory Pecans

Prep Time: 5 min   Start to Finish: 15 min   16 Servings

2 cups pecan halves
2 medium green onions, chopped (2 tablespoons)
2 tablespoons butter or margarine, melted
1 tablespoon soy sauce
¼ teaspoon ground red pepper (cayenne)

1 Heat oven to 300°F. In small bowl, mix all ingredients. In ungreased 15×10×1-inch pan, spread mixture in single layer.

2 Bake uncovered 10 minutes or until pecans are toasted. Serve warm, or cool completely. Store in airtight container at room temperature up to 3 weeks.

1 Serving: Calories 110 (Calories from Fat 90); Total Fat 10g (Saturated Fat 1.5g); Cholesterol 0mg; Sodium 65mg; Total Carbohydrate 2g (Dietary Fiber 1g); Protein 1g

Italian Sautéed Olives

Prep Time: 5 min ■ Start to Finish: 15 min ■ 20 Servings

2 tablespoons olive or vegetable oil
2 tablespoons chopped fresh parsley
1 medium green onion, chopped (1 tablespoon)
1 teaspoon crushed red pepper flakes
2 cloves garlic, finely chopped
1 cup kalamata olives (8 oz), drained and pitted
1 cup Greek green olives (8 oz), drained and pitted
1 cup Gaeta olives (8 oz), drained and pitted

1 In 10-inch skillet, heat oil over medium heat. Cook parsley, onion, red pepper and garlic in oil about 4 minutes, stirring frequently, until garlic just begins to become golden brown.

2 Stir in olives. Cover; cook about 5 minutes, stirring occasionally, until olives are tender and skins begin to wrinkle.

1 Serving (6 olives each): Calories 40 (Calories from Fat 35); Total Fat 4g (Saturated Fat 0.5g); Cholesterol 0mg; Sodium 220mg; Total Carbohydrate 1g (Dietary Fiber 1g); Protein 0g

Create an easy yet impressive appetizer platter by pairing the olives with a sliced baguette loaf and wedges of cheese like Asiago, Parmesan, manchego, Gouda, blue and Brie.

Bacon-Turkey Bites

Chicken-Ham Bites

Spicy Chicken Wings

Mini Salmon Wraps

Ham and Roasted Red Pepper Bites

Veggie Tortilla Roll-Ups

Sesame Toast–Vegetable Bites

Antipasto Pizzettes

Olive and Herb Deviled Eggs

Stuffed Sweet Banana Peppers

Stuffed Baby Portabella Mushrooms

Olive-Cheese Balls

Chipotle Cheesecake

Cheese and Fruit Kabobs with Cranberry Dip

Fruit Bruschetta

2

lazy day buffet

Begin these up to 24 hours in advance, then finish the next day.

Bacon-Turkey Bites

Prep Time: 25 min   ▦   Start to Finish: 1 hr 10 min   ▦   24 to 30 Appetizers

1 small turkey breast tenderloin ($1/2$ to $3/4$ lb), cut into $1/2$- to $3/4$-inch cubes
$1/2$ cup honey mustard dressing
8 to 10 slices bacon, cut crosswise into thirds
$1/2$ cup jellied cranberry sauce
2 tablespoons honey mustard dressing
$1/2$ teaspoon ground mustard
1 to 2 tablespoons chopped fresh chives

1 In shallow bowl, mix turkey and $1/2$ cup honey mustard dressing. Cover and refrigerate 30 minutes to marinate.

2 Remove turkey from marinade; discard marinade. Wrap bacon piece around each turkey piece; secure with toothpick. Place on ungreased broiler pan rack.

3 Broil with tops 4 to 6 inches from heat 8 to 12 minutes, turning once, until turkey is no longer pink in center and bacon begins to look crisp.

4 Meanwhile, in 1-quart saucepan, mix cranberry sauce, 2 tablespoons honey mustard dressing and mustard. Cook over low heat, stirring occasionally, just until melted and well blended; cool slightly. Just before serving, sprinkle with chives. Serve turkey bites with sauce.

1 Appetizer: Calories 50 (Calories from Fat 25); Total Fat 3g (Saturated Fat 1g); Cholesterol 10mg; Sodium 80mg; Total Carbohydrate 3g (Dietary Fiber 0g); Protein 3g

Do Ahead: Prepare and bake these turkey bites up to 24 hours in advance. Cover tightly and refrigerate. Just before serving, heat at 375°F about 15 minutes or until hot.

Chicken-Ham Bites

Prep Time: 30 min ▪ Start to Finish: 1 hr 15 min ▪ 36 Appetizers

2 boneless skinless chicken breasts, cut into ½- to ¾-inch pieces (36 pieces)
½ cup Italian dressing
14 to 16 cremini mushrooms, cut into ¼-inch slices
6 oz sliced cooked deli ham, cut into 1-inch-wide strips
4 fresh basil leaves, finely sliced

1 In shallow bowl, place chicken pieces. Pour dressing over chicken. Cover and refrigerate 30 minutes to marinate.

2 Heat oven to 425°F. Line 15×10-inch pan with foil. Spray foil with cooking spray. Place 1 chicken piece on each mushroom slice; wrap with ham strip. Place seam side down (mushroom on bottom) in pan. Drizzle with remaining marinade in bowl.

3 Bake 10 to 12 minutes or until juice of chicken is clear when center of thickest part is cut (170°F). Place basil on top of each bite. Serve with cocktail toothpicks if desired.

1 Appetizer: Calories 35 (Calories from Fat 20); Total Fat 2g (Saturated Fat 0g); Cholesterol 5mg; Sodium 90mg; Total Carbohydrate 1g (Dietary Fiber 0g); Protein 3g

Do Ahead: Bake these tasty appetizers up to 24 hours in advance. Transfer them to an ovenproof baking dish; cover and refrigerate. When ready to serve, reheat at 350°F for 20 to 25 minutes.

Spicy Chicken Wings

Prep Time: 25 min ▪ Start to Finish: 2 hr 15 min ▪ 40 Appetizers

20 chicken wings (about 4 lbs)
1/4 cup dry sherry or chicken broth
1/4 cup oyster sauce
1/4 cup honey
3 tablespoons chopped fresh cilantro
2 tablespoons chili sauce
2 tablespoons grated lime peel
4 medium green onions, chopped (1/4 cup)
3 cloves garlic, finely chopped

1 Cut each chicken wing at joints to make 3 pieces; discard tip. Cut off and discard excess skin.

2 In resealable heavy-duty plastic food-storage bag or large glass bowl, mix remaining ingredients. Add chicken to marinade. Seal bag; turn to coat. Refrigerate at least 1 hour but no longer than 24 hours, turning once.

3 Heat oven to 375°F. In ungreased 15×10-inch pan, place chicken. Bake uncovered 30 minutes, stirring frequently. Bake about 20 minutes longer or until juice of chicken is clear when thickest part is cut to bone (180°F).

1 Appetizer: Calories 60 (Calories from Fat 25); Total Fat 3g (Saturated Fat 1g); Cholesterol 15mg; Sodium 75mg; Total Carbohydrate 3g (Dietary Fiber 0g); Protein 5g

Do Ahead: Prepare and bake these zesty wings up to 24 hours ahead. Cover with aluminum foil and refrigerate. To reheat, place the covered pan in the oven at 350°F for 20 to 25 minutes or until chicken is heated through.

Mini Salmon Wraps

Prep Time: 20 min ▪ Start to Finish: 30 min ▪ 48 Mini Wraps

2 packages (3 oz each) cream cheese, softened
2 tablespoons horseradish sauce
6 spinach, tomato or plain flour tortillas (8 to 10 inch)
1 medium cucumber, peeled, finely chopped (1 cup)
1/4 cup sour cream
1/4 cup chopped fresh dill weed
1/4 cup finely chopped red or yellow onion
8 oz salmon lox, cut into thin strips

1 In small bowl, mix cream cheese and horseradish sauce. Spread cream cheese mixture evenly over tortillas.

2 In small bowl, mix cucumber, sour cream, dill weed and onion; spread over cream cheese mixture. Arrange salmon strips over cucumber mixture. Roll up tortillas tightly.

3 Cover and refrigerate wraps 10 minutes or until ready to serve. Cut each wrap into 8 pieces.

1 Mini Wrap: Calories 40 (Calories from Fat 20); Total Fat 2g (Saturated Fat 1g); Cholesterol 5mg; Sodium 75mg; Total Carbohydrate 3g (Dietary Fiber 0g); Protein 2g

Do Ahead: These sophisticated wraps can be made up to 24 hours ahead; cover with plastic wrap and refrigerate.

Ham and Roasted Red Pepper Bites

Prep Time: 25 min ▮ Start to Finish: 2 hr 25 min ▮ 25 Appetizers

1 package (2.5 oz) thinly sliced ham
3 tablespoons reduced-fat garden vegetable cream cheese
  (from 8-oz container)
1 package (²/₃ oz) fresh basil leaves
¹/₃ cup roasted red bell peppers (from 7-oz jar), patted dry
5 pieces (5¹/₂ inches long) string cheese

1 Stack 2 slices ham on work surface; pat dry with paper towel. Spread evenly with 1¹/₂ to 2 teaspoons cream cheese. Top with basil leaves to within 1 inch of top edge. Cut bell pepper into 1-inch strips; cut to fit width of ham. Place pepper strip across bottom edge of ham. Place cheese piece above pepper on basil leaves; trim to fit.

2 Beginning at bottom, roll up securely. Wrap in plastic wrap. Repeat with remaining ingredients to make 5 rolls. Refrigerate 2 hours.

3 Unwrap rolls; place seam sides down. Cut each roll into 5 pieces with sharp serrated knife. If desired, pierce each roll with 5 evenly spaced toothpicks before cutting.

1 Appetizer: Calories 40 (Calories from Fat 20); Total Fat 2g (Saturated Fat 1g); Cholesterol 10mg; Sodium 85mg; Total Carbohydrate 1g (Dietary Fiber 0g); Protein 4g

Do Ahead: Save yourself some time by assembling the rolls up to 24 hours ahead. Slice them just before serving.

Veggie Tortilla Roll-Ups

Prep Time: 15 min ▪ Start to Finish: 3 hr 15 min ▪ About 30 servings

1 package (3 oz) cream cheese, softened
½ cup sour cream
½ cup finely shredded Cheddar cheese (2 oz)
¼ cup finely chopped red bell pepper
2 tablespoons sliced ripe olives, chopped
1 tablespoon chopped fresh parsley
3 flavored or plain flour tortillas (8 to 10 inch)

1 In medium bowl, mix all ingredients except tortillas. Spread about ½ cup of the cheese mixture over one side of each tortilla. Tightly roll tortilla up. Repeat with the remaining tortillas and cheese mixture.

2 Wrap each tortilla roll individually in plastic wrap. Refrigerate at least 3 hours but no longer than 24 hours. To serve, cut each tortilla roll into 1-inch slices.

1 Serving: Calories 40 (Calories from Fat 25); Total Fat 3g (Saturated Fat 2g); Cholesterol 10mg; Sodium 45mg; Total Carbohydrate 3g (Dietary Fiber 0g); Protein 1g

For more flavor and variety, use a combination of flavored tortillas for the roll-ups. Spinach and tomato, for example, are a perfect pair on a holiday appetizer platter.

Sesame Toast–Vegetable Bites

Prep Time: 40 min   ▪   Start to Finish: 40 min   ▪   24 Appetizers

1 can (8 oz) refrigerated crescent dinner rolls (8 rolls)
1 egg, beaten
1 teaspoon sesame seed
4 oz cream cheese (from 8-oz package), softened
$1/2$ teaspoon grated lemon peel
$1/4$ teaspoon dried dill weed
12 fresh sugar snap peas, cut crosswise in half
$1/2$ medium red bell pepper, cut into 24 ($1^1/2$-inch) strips
24 small broccoli or cauliflower florets
1 medium carrot, cut lengthwise in half, then cut crosswise into 12 slices
(24 pieces)

1 Heat oven to 375°F. Unroll dough into 12×8-inch rectangle; press perforations to seal. Brush dough with egg; sprinkle with sesame seed. Cut dough lengthwise into 4 strips. Cut each strip crosswise into 6 pieces. On ungreased cookie sheet, place pieces 2 inches apart.

2 Bake 6 to 8 minutes or until golden brown. Remove from cookie sheet to cooling rack. Cool completely, about 10 minutes.

3 Meanwhile, in small bowl, mix cream cheese, lemon peel and dill weed until smooth.

4 Spread cream cheese mixture over cooled toasts. Arrange 1 piece of each vegetable on each toast.

1 Appetizer: Calories 60 (Calories from Fat 35); Total Fat 4g (Saturated Fat 2g); Cholesterol 15mg; Sodium 95mg; Total Carbohydrate 5g (Dietary Fiber 0g); Protein 2g

Do Ahead: A day or two ahead, cut up the veggies, mix the cream cheese spread and bake the toasts, then assemble just before serving.

Antipasto Pizzettes

Prep Time: 30 min ▮ Start to Finish: 40 min ▮ 24 Pizzettes

2 cups Original Bisquick® mix
1/2 cup water
2 tablespoons olive or vegetable oil
2 teaspoons dried basil leaves
1/2 cup shredded mozzarella cheese (2 oz)
1/4 cup basil pesto
24 slices plum (Roma) tomatoes (about 3 small)
24 slices pepperoni
24 slices banana peppers or sliced pepperoncini peppers (bottled Italian peppers), if desired

1 Heat oven to 450°F. Lightly spray cookie sheet with cooking spray. In medium bowl, stir Bisquick mix, water, oil and 1 teaspoon of the basil with fork or wire whisk until soft dough forms. On lightly floured surface, knead dough 10 times.

2 Roll dough into 12-inch circle, about 1/4 inch thick. Using 2-inch round cutter, cut out dough rounds; reroll dough once to get 24 rounds. Place on cookie sheet.

3 Bake 8 to 10 minutes or until light golden brown. Cool completely, about 15 minutes. Store in airtight container until serving.

4 Meanwhile, in small bowl, mix cheese and remaining 1 teaspoon basil. To serve, spread about 1/2 teaspoon pesto on each biscuit round. Top each with 1 slice tomato, 1 slice pepperoni and cheese mixture. Top with sliced pepper. Serve at room temperature.

1 Pizzette: Calories 100 (Calories from Fat 60); Total Fat 7g (Saturated Fat 2g); Cholesterol 5mg; Sodium 290mg; Total Carbohydrate 7g (Dietary Fiber 0g); Protein 3g

Do Ahead: Bake and freeze the biscuit rounds up to a week ahead. Just warm thawed rounds on a cookie sheet at 450°F for 2 to 4 minutes and serve.

Olive and Herb Deviled Eggs

Prep Time: 1 hr ▮ Start to Finish: 1 hr ▮ 16 Deviled Eggs

8 eggs
1/3 cup mayonnaise or salad dressing
2 tablespoons finely chopped parsley
2 tablespoons finely chopped fresh marjoram leaves
2 tablespoons finely chopped fresh chives
1/2 teaspoon garlic-pepper blend
1/2 cup chopped ripe olives
8 pitted ripe olives
Fresh parsley or marjoram sprigs or leaves, if desired

1 In 3-quart saucepan, place eggs in single layer; add enough cold water to cover eggs by 1 inch. Cover; heat to boiling. Remove from heat; let stand covered 15 minutes. Drain. Immediately place eggs in cold water with ice cubes or run cold water over eggs until completely cooled.

2 To remove shell from each egg, crackle it by tapping gently all over; roll between hands to loosen. Peel, starting at large end. With rippled vegetable cutter or sharp knife, cut each egg in half lengthwise. Carefully remove yolks and place in small bowl; mash with fork. Reserve egg white halves.

3 Stir mayonnaise, chopped herbs, garlic-pepper blend and chopped olives into mashed yolks. Carefully spoon mixture into egg white halves, mounding lightly.

4 Cut whole pitted olives into slices; top each egg half with olive slices. Garnish with small herb sprigs or leaves.

1 Deviled Egg: Calories 80 (Calories from Fat 60); Total Fat 7g (Saturated Fat 1.5g); Cholesterol 110mg; Sodium 110mg; Total Carbohydrate 0g (Dietary Fiber 0g); Protein 3g

Instead of an olive slice, top each egg half with a cherry tomato wedge. To make ahead, store stuffed eggs tightly covered in the fridge up to 24 hours before serving.

Stuffed Sweet Banana Peppers

Prep Time: 35 min ▮ Start to Finish: 35 min ▮ 12 Appetizers

12 small (2 to 2¹/₂ inches) sweet banana wax peppers (from 16-oz jar)
¹/₃ cup chive-and-onion cream cheese spread (from 8-oz container)
¹/₄ cup finely chopped pastrami

1 Cut small slice from flat side of each pepper, keeping stem intact. Carefully remove seeds. Drain on paper towels.

2 In small bowl, mix cream cheese and pastrami. Spoon into peppers. Wipe any cheese mixture from outside of peppers.

1 Appetizer: Calories 60 (Calories from Fat 35); Total Fat 4g (Saturated Fat 1g); Cholesterol 5mg; Sodium 240mg; Total Carbohydrate 5g (Dietary Fiber 0g); Protein 2g

Do Ahead: These yummy peppers can be filled and refrigerated, covered, for up to 24 hours.

Stuffed Baby Portabella Mushrooms

Prep Time: 20 min ▪ Start to Finish: 40 min ▪ 26 Mushrooms

2 packages (5 oz each) fresh baby
    portabella mushrooms or large
    regular white mushrooms
2 tablespoons butter or margarine
³/₄ cup chopped red onion
1 cup frozen chopped broccoli,
    thawed, drained
¹/₄ cup garlic & herb bread crumbs

1 package (5.2 oz) Boursin cheese
    with garlic and herbs
¹/₂ teaspoon dried basil leaves
¹/₂ teaspoon dried oregano leaves
¹/₂ teaspoon garlic salt
¹/₂ teaspoon pepper
1 tablespoon chopped roasted red
    bell peppers (from a jar)

1 Heat oven to 350°F. Carefully remove stems from mushrooms. Chop enough stems to measure ¹/₂ cup.

2 In 10-inch skillet, melt butter over medium heat. Cook onion and broccoli in butter 2 minutes, stirring occasionally. Stir in mushroom stems. Cook about 2 minutes, stirring occasionally, until broccoli is crisp-tender. Cool slightly. Stir in bread crumbs, cheese, basil, oregano, garlic salt and pepper.

3 Spoon vegetable mixture evenly into mushroom caps, mounding slightly. In ungreased 15×10-inch pan, place stuffed mushrooms. Garnish each with bell pepper pieces.

4 Bake uncovered 12 to 15 minutes or until filling is light golden brown.

1 Mushroom: Calories 40 (Calories from Fat 25); Total Fat 3g (Saturated Fat 1.5g); Cholesterol 10mg; Sodium 65mg; Total Carbohydrate 2g (Dietary Fiber 0g); Protein 1g

Do Ahead: Prepare these tasty mushrooms through step 3; store tightly covered in refrigerator up to 24 hours before baking and serving.

Olive-Cheese Balls

Prep Time: 30 min ▪ Start to Finish: 1 hr 50 min ▪ 48 Appetizers

2 cups shredded sharp natural Cheddar cheese (8 oz)
1¼ cups all-purpose flour
½ cup butter or margarine, melted
48 small pimiento-stuffed olives, drained, patted dry

1 Heat oven to 400°F. In large bowl, stir together cheese and flour. Stir in butter thoroughly. (If dough seems dry, work with hands.)

2 Mold 1 teaspoon dough around each olive; shape into ball. On ungreased cookie sheet, place balls 2 inches apart. Cover and refrigerate at least 1 hour but no longer than 24 hours.

3 Bake 15 to 20 minutes or until light brown.

1 Serving: Calories 55 (Calories from Fat 35); Total Fat 4g (Saturated Fat 1g); Cholesterol 5mg; Sodium 130mg; Total Carbohydrate 3g (Dietary Fiber 0g); Protein 2g

Do Ahead: Place unbaked olive-cheese balls on ungreased cookie sheet. Freeze at least 2 hours until firm. Place balls in plastic freezer bags. Seal, label and freeze up to 3 months. Heat oven to 400°F. Place cheese balls 2 inches apart on ungreased cookie sheet. Bake about 20 minutes or until hot.

Chipotle Cheesecake

Prep Time: 20 min ▪ Start to Finish: 5 hr 5 min ▪ 36 servings

1 cup crushed tortilla chips
3 tablespoons butter or margarine, melted
2 packages (8 oz each) cream cheese, softened
2 eggs
1/2 cup sour cream
2 cups shredded Colby-Monterey Jack cheese blend (8 oz)
1/4 cup chopped drained roasted red bell peppers (from 7-oz jar)
4 chipotle chiles in adobo sauce (from 7-oz can), seeded, chopped
    (2 tablespoons)
1 tablespoon adobo sauce from can of chipotle chiles
Large tortilla chips, if desired

1 Heat oven to 375°F. In medium bowl, mix tortilla chips and butter until well blended. Press evenly in bottom of springform pan, 9×3 inches. Bake about 8 minutes or until golden brown.

2 Reduce oven temperature to 325°F. In large bowl, beat cream cheese with electric mixer on medium speed until smooth. Add eggs; beat until well blended. Beat in sour cream. Stir in cheese, bell peppers, chipotle chiles and adobo sauce until well blended. Spoon evenly over crust.

3 Bake uncovered 40 to 45 minutes or until center is set. Run knife around edge of cheesecake to loosen. Cool completely at room temperature, about 2 hours. Cover and refrigerate at least 2 hours but no longer than 24 hours. Remove side of pan. Serve cheesecake with tortilla chips.

1 Serving: Calories 100 (Calories from Fat 80); Total Fat 9g (Saturated Fat 5g); Cholesterol 35mg; Sodium 125mg; Total Carbohydrate 2g (Dietary Fiber 0g); Protein 3g

Make it easy for your guests to help themselves to this savory cheesecake from your appetizer buffet. Cut a 4-inch diameter circle in the center of the cheesecake before cutting it into wedges, so guests can easily cut short wedges from 2 rings of cheesecake instead of longer wedges.

Cheese and Fruit Kabobs with Cranberry Dip

Prep Time: 40 min ▮ Start to Finish: 40 min ▮ 12 Kabobs

Kabobs

12 (1/2-inch) cubes Gouda cheese (about 6 oz)

12 (1/2-inch) cubes fontina cheese (about 6 oz)

12 (1/2-inch) cubes Cheddar cheese (about 6 oz)

12 small strawberries or 6 large strawberries, cut in half

2 kiwifruit, peeled and cut into 12 pieces

12 fresh or canned pineapple cubes

12 wooden skewers (6 inch)

Dip

2/3 cup strawberry cream cheese spread (from 8-oz container)

1/4 cup frozen (thawed) cranberry-orange relish (from 10-oz container)

1/4 cup frozen (thawed) whipped topping

1 Thread cheese and fruit alternately on each of twelve 6-inch wooden skewers.

2 In small bowl, beat cream cheese and cranberry relish with electric mixer on medium speed until smooth. Fold in whipped topping. Spoon into serving bowl. Serve kabobs with dip.

1 Kabob: Calories 225 (Calories from Fat 145); Total Fat 16g (Saturated Fat 10g); Cholesterol 55mg; Sodium 340mg; Total Carbohydrate 8g (Dietary Fiber 1g); Protein 12g

Do Ahead: Prepare the dip a day ahead; cover and refrigerate. Cut the cheese and fruit the day ahead. Store them all separately in plastic bags in the refrigerator. Assemble the kabobs up to 2 hours before serving; cover and refrigerate.

Fruit Bruschetta

Prep Time: 20 min ▮ Start to Finish: 20 min ▮ 28 Servings

1 package (10.75 oz) frozen pound cake loaf, thawed, cut into fourteen $\frac{1}{2}$-inch slices
$\frac{2}{3}$ cup cream cheese spread with strawberries, raspberries or pineapple (from 8-oz container)

1 can (11 oz) mandarin orange segments, drained
Assorted bite-size pieces fresh fruit (kiwifruit, strawberry, raspberry, pear, apple)
Chocolate-flavor syrup, if desired
Toasted coconut or sliced almonds, if desired

1 Set oven control to broil. Place pound cake slices on rack in broiler pan. Broil with tops 4 to 5 inches from heat 3 to 5 minutes, turning once, until light golden brown.

2 Spread each slice with about 2 teaspoons cream cheese. Cut slices diagonally in half to make 28 pieces. Top with orange segments and desired fruit. Drizzle with syrup; sprinkle with coconut. Arrange on serving platter.

1 Serving: Calories 70 (Calories from Fat 23); Total Fat 4g (Saturated Fat 2g); Cholesterol 15mg; Sodium 20mg; Total Carbohydrate 9g (Dietary Fiber 1g); Protein 1g

Do Ahead: Toast the pound cake up to a day ahead of time. You can assemble the bruschetta up to 4 hours before your party. Cover and refrigerate until serving time.

Ham Salad in Cucumber Cups

Spicy Sesame Chicken Strips

Shrimp and Red Potato Snacks

Gingered Shrimp

Easy Phyllo Egg Rolls

Black Bean and Corn Wonton Cups

Savory Stuffed Mushrooms

Roasted Pepper–Tomato Crostini

Pea Pod Roll-Ups

Potato Bites

Sweet Potato Fries with Easy Fruit Salsa

Bacon-Wrapped Figs

Blue Cheese–Stuffed Grapes

Fruit Kabobs with Tropical Fruit Coulis

Cheesy Apple Polenta Bites

3

light bites

Ham Salad in Cucumber Cups

Prep Time: 20 min ▪ Start to Finish: 20 min ▪ 24 Appetizers

2 seedless cucumbers
¾ cup ham salad
4 lemon slices, cut into wedges, if desired

1 Cut tapered ends from cucumbers. Peel lengthwise strips of peel every half inch with citrus stripper. Cut cucumbers into ⅝- to ¾-inch slices. Make indentation in center of each slice, without going all the way through, by scooping with small melon ball cutter.

2 Fill each indentation with about 1 teaspoon ham salad. Top each appetizer with lemon wedge.

1 Appetizer: Calories 15 (Calories from Fat 10); Total Fat 1g (Saturated Fat 0g); Cholesterol 0mg; Sodium 50mg; Total Carbohydrate 0g (Dietary Fiber 0g); Protein 0g

Spicy Sesame Chicken Strips

Prep Time: 20 min ▪ Start to Finish: 35 min ▪ 16 Appetizers

4 boneless skinless chicken breasts (about 1¼ lb)
½ cup hoisin sauce
½ cup orange marmalade
2 tablespoons honey
¼ to ½ teaspoon ground red pepper (cayenne)
1 teaspoon finely chopped gingerroot
1 clove garlic, finely chopped
8 red pearl onions, peeled, halved or 16 grape tomatoes
8 whole green onions
1 tablespoon sesame seed, toasted,* if desired
16 wooden skewers (8 to 10 inch)

1 Heat oven to 425°F. Line 15×10-inch pan with foil. Cut each chicken breast half lengthwise into 4 strips. Thread chicken strip on each skewer, leaving ½-inch space on pointed end. Place skewers in pan; set aside.

2 In medium bowl, mix remaining ingredients except tomatoes, onions and sesame seed. Reserve ½ cup hoisin mixture. Spoon remaining hoisin mixture into small serving bowl; cover and refrigerate until serving. Brush chicken with ½ cup reserved hoisin mixture.

3 Bake 12 to 15 minutes, brushing chicken occasionally with pan drippings, until chicken is no longer pink in center. Thread 1 onion half on end of each skewer. To serve, line serving platter with onions; arrange skewers on onions. Sprinkle sesame seed over chicken. Serve with remaining hoisin mixture (heated if desired).

1 Appetizer: Calories 70 (Calories from Fat 10); Total Fat 1g (Saturated Fat 0g); Cholesterol 20mg; Sodium 110mg; Total Carbohydrate 9g (Dietary Fiber 1g); Protein 7g

*To toast sesame seed, bake uncovered in ungreased shallow pan in 350°F oven 8 to 10 minutes, stirring occasionally, until golden brown.

Shrimp and Red Potato Snacks

Prep Time: 15 min   Start to Finish: 30 min   20 Snacks

5 small red potatoes, about 1½
   inches in diameter
2 teaspoons olive oil
¼ teaspoon salt
10 cooked deveined peeled
   medium shrimp, thawed
   if frozen, tail shells removed

¼ cup reduced-fat garlic-and-
   herbs spreadable cheese
   (from 4-oz container)
Dill weed sprigs

1 Heat oven to 400°F. Line cookie sheet with foil or cooking parchment paper; lightly spray with cooking spray. Cut each potato into four ¼-inch slices, trimming off round ends. Coat with oil and salt. Place on cookie sheet.

2 Bake 15 to 18 minutes or until tender and edges begin to turn light golden brown. Cool about 10 minutes.

3 Meanwhile, cut each shrimp lengthwise in half. To serve, spread about ½ teaspoon cheese on each potato slice; top with shrimp half and small dill weed sprig.

1 Snack: Calories 45 (Calories from Fat 10); Total Fat 1g (Saturated Fat 0g); Cholesterol 5mg; Sodium 50mg; Total Carbohydrate 7g (Dietary Fiber 0g); Protein 1g

Do Ahead: Slice and bake the potatoes the day before. Cover and refrigerate until serving time. It couldn't be easier!

Gingered Shrimp

Prep Time: 20 min ▪ Start to Finish: 2 hr 20 min ▪ 40 to 45 Shrimp

1½ lb cooked deveined peeled medium shrimp, thawed if frozen
¼ cup soy sauce
2 teaspoons chopped gingerroot
¼ cup white vinegar
2 tablespoons sugar
2 tablespoons sake or apple juice
1½ teaspoons salt
2 or 3 medium green onions, thinly sliced (2 to 3 tablespoons)

1 In 11×7-inch glass or plastic container, arrange shrimp in single layer. In 1-quart saucepan, heat soy sauce to boiling over high heat. Stir in gingerroot; reduce heat to medium. Simmer uncovered about 5 minutes or until liquid is reduced by half. Stir in vinegar, sugar, sake and salt; pour over shrimp. Cover; refrigerate 2 to 3 hours.

2 Remove shrimp from marinade with slotted spoon; arrange on serving plate. Discard marinade. Sprinkle onions over shrimp. Serve shrimp with toothpicks.

1 Shrimp: Calories 15 (Calories from Fat 0); Total Fat 0g (Saturated Fat 0g); Cholesterol 35mg; Sodium 85mg; Total Carbohydrate 0g (Dietary Fiber 0g); Protein 4g

Make it easy on your guests. Because these shrimp will be eaten with the fingers, purchase shrimp with the tail on for a prettier look. Provide a small bowl for the tails.

Easy Phyllo Egg Rolls

Prep Time: 30 min ▪ Start to Finish: 50 min ▪ 18 Egg Rolls

1 lb ground turkey breast
4 cups coleslaw mix (from 16-oz bag)
3 tablespoons soy sauce
1 teaspoon grated gingerroot
½ teaspoon five-spice powder
1 small onion, chopped (¼ cup)
2 cloves garlic, finely chopped
18 sheets frozen phyllo (filo) pastry (18x14 inch), thawed
Cooking spray

1 Heat oven to 350°F. In 10-inch skillet, cook turkey over medium-high heat, stirring occasionally, until no longer pink; drain. Stir in remaining ingredients except phyllo and cooking spray. Cook 2 to 3 minutes, stirring occasionally, until coleslaw mix is wilted.

2 Cover phyllo sheets with plastic wrap, then with damp towel to keep them from drying out. Place 1 phyllo sheet on cutting board; spray with cooking spray. Repeat with 2 more phyllo sheets to make stack of 3 sheets. Cut stack of phyllo crosswise into thirds to make 3 rectangles, about 14×6 inches.

3 Place ¼ cup turkey mixture on short end of each rectangle; roll up, folding in edges of phyllo. Place roll, seam side down, on ungreased cookie sheet. Repeat with remaining phyllo and turkey mixture. Spray rolls with cooking spray. Bake 15 to 20 minutes or until light golden brown. Serve warm.

1 Egg Roll: Calories 100 (Calories from Fat 0); Total Fat 0g (Saturated Fat 0g); Cholesterol 15mg; Sodium 240mg; Total Carbohydrate 15g (Dietary Fiber 1g); Protein 8g

Black Bean and Corn Wonton Cups

Prep Time: 25 min   Start to Finish: 35 min   36 Appetizers

36 wonton skins
2/3 cup chunky-style salsa
1/4 cup chopped fresh cilantro
1/2 teaspoon ground cumin
1/2 teaspoon chili powder
1 can (15.25 oz) whole kernel corn, drained
1 can (15 oz) black beans, drained, rinsed
1/4 cup sour cream
Cilantro sprigs, if desired

1 Heat oven to 350°F. Gently fit 1 wonton skin into each of 36 small muffin cups, 1³/₄×1 inch, pressing against bottom and side. Bake 8 to 10 minutes or until light golden brown. Remove from pan; cool on cooling rack.

2 Mix remaining ingredients except sour cream and cilantro sprigs. Just before serving, spoon bean mixture into wonton cups. Top each with 1/2 teaspoon sour cream. Garnish each with cilantro sprig.

1 Serving: Calories 55 (Calories from Fat 10); Total Fat 1g (Saturated Fat 0g); Cholesterol 5mg; Sodium 90mg; Total Carbohydrate 10g (Dietary Fiber 1g); Protein 2g

Get a head start on your party by baking the wontons and making the filling 2 days before. Fill and garnish wonton cups just before serving.

Savory Stuffed Mushrooms

Prep Time: 20 min ▪ Start to Finish: 40 min ▪ 36 Mushrooms

36 medium mushrooms (1 lb)
2 tablespoons butter or margarine
1 small onion, chopped (¼ cup)
¼ cup chopped red bell pepper
1½ cups soft bread crumbs (about 2½ slices bread)
1½ teaspoons chopped fresh or ½ teaspoon dried thyme leaves
½ teaspoon salt
¼ teaspoon ground turmeric
¼ teaspoon pepper

1 Heat oven to 350°F. Lightly spray rectangular pan, 11×7 inches, with cooking spray. Remove mushroom stems from mushroom caps. Finely chop enough stems to measure ⅓ cup. Reserve mushroom caps.

2 In 10-inch skillet over medium-high heat, melt butter. Cook mushroom stems, onion and bell pepper in butter about 5 minutes, stirring occasionally, until tender; remove from heat. Stir in remaining ingredients.

3 Fill mushroom caps with bread crumb mixture. Place mushrooms, filled sides up, in baking dish. Bake uncovered 15 minutes.

4 Set oven control to broil. Broil with tops 3 to 4 inches from heat about 2 minutes or until light brown. Serve warm.

1 Mushroom: Calories 30 (Calories from Fat 10); Total Fat 1g (Saturated Fat 0g); Cholesterol 0mg; Sodium 80mg; Total Carbohydrate 4g (Dietary Fiber 0g); Protein 1g

Roasted Pepper–Tomato Crostini

Prep Time: 15 min ▪ Start to Finish: 25 min ▪ 18 Crostini

18 slices Italian bread, ½ inch thick
2 large tomatoes, diced (2 cups)
1 jar (7 oz) roasted red bell peppers, drained, chopped
¼ cup chopped fresh basil leaves
1 tablespoon balsamic vinegar
¼ teaspoon salt
⅓ cup shredded mozzarella cheese

1 Heat oven to 375°F. Place bread on cookie sheet. Bake about 5 minutes or until toasted.

2 Mix tomatoes, bell peppers, basil, vinegar and salt. Spread tomato mixture on bread. Top each slice with about 1 teaspoon cheese.

3 Bake about 5 minutes or until cheese is melted. Serve hot.

1 Crostini: Calories 65 (Calories from Fat 10); Total Fat 1g (Saturated Fat 0g); Cholesterol 0mg; Sodium 160mg; Total Carbohydrate 12g (Dietary Fiber 1g); Protein 3g

Do Ahead: It's a snap! You can prepare the tomato topping and bake the bread several hours ahead. Just before serving, spread the topping on the bread and bake as directed.

Pea Pod Roll-Ups

Prep Time: 20 min ▪ Start to Finish: 20 min ▪ 24 Roll-Ups

3 cups water
6 oz fresh snow pea pods (24 to 30 pea pods)
⅓ cup salmon cream cheese spread (from 8-oz container)
1 to 2 teaspoons chopped fresh dill weed
24 pieces (½x¼ inch) red bell pepper, cucumber, carrot or red onion

1 In 1½- to 2-quart saucepan, heat water to boiling; add pea pods. Cook uncovered 1 to 2 minutes or until bright green; drain. Immediately rinse with cold water; drain. Dry with paper towels.

2 Spread cream cheese over each pea pod; sprinkle with dill weed. Place 1 piece of bell pepper on center of each pea pod; bring ends of pea pod over filling, overlapping in center. Secure with toothpick.

1 Roll-Up: Calories 15 (Calories from Fat 10); Total Fat 1g (Saturated Fat 0.5g); Cholesterol 0mg; Sodium 25mg; Total Carbohydrate 0g (Dietary Fiber 0g); Protein 0g

If you use carrots, cook them with the pea pods to soften them slightly.

Potato Bites

Prep Time: 40 min ▪ Start to Finish: 55 min ▪ 44 Appetizers

1 bag (20 oz) refrigerated mashed potatoes (about 2 cups)
1 cup frozen sweet peas (from 1-lb bag)
⅓ cup chopped red onion
1 teaspoon ground coriander
½ teaspoon ground cumin
¼ teaspoon salt
⅛ teaspoon ground red pepper (cayenne)
1 cup unseasoned dry bread crumbs
2 eggs
2 tablespoons fat-free (skim) milk
Cooking spray
Tomato chutney or chunky-style salsa, if desired

1 Heat oven to 400°F. Line cookie sheet with foil or cooking parchment paper; spray foil or paper with cooking spray. In medium bowl, mix potatoes, peas, onion, coriander, cumin, salt and red pepper.

2 In shallow bowl, place bread crumbs. In another shallow bowl, beat eggs and milk with fork or wire whisk. Shape potato mixture by tablespoonfuls into about 1-inch balls. Roll balls in bread crumbs to coat, then dip into egg mixture and coat again with bread crumbs. Place on cookie sheet. Spray tops of balls with cooking spray.

3 Bake 10 to 14 minutes or until light golden brown and hot. Serve warm with chutney.

1 Appetizer: Calories 30 (Calories from Fat 10); Total Fat 1g (Saturated Fat 0g); Cholesterol 10mg; Sodium 65mg; Total Carbohydrate 4g (Dietary Fiber 0g); Protein 1g

The easy way to make potato balls that are all the same size? Use a small ice-cream scoop. To serve, skewer each bite with a colorful, fringed toothpick.

Sweet Potato Fries with Easy Fruit Salsa

Prep Time: 15 min ▪ Start to Finish: 45 min ▪ About 60 Appetizers

3 lb sweet potatoes (about 3 inches in diameter)
½ teaspoon garlic salt
1 tablespoon olive or vegetable oil
1 jar (16 oz) thick-and-chunky salsa
1 cup frozen sliced peaches, thawed, chopped
1 can (8 oz) pineapple tidbits, drained

1 Heat oven to 375°F. Spray large cookie sheets with cooking spray. Cut potatoes into ¼-inch slices; arrange in single layer on cookie sheets. Sprinkle with garlic salt; drizzle with oil.

2 Bake 10 minutes; turn. Bake 15 to 20 minutes longer or until potatoes are golden brown.

3 Mix remaining ingredients. Serve chips with salsa.

1 Appetizer: Calories 15 (Calories from Fat 0); Total Fat 0g (Saturated Fat 0g); Cholesterol 0mg; Sodium 30mg; Total Carbohydrate 5g (Dietary Fiber 1g); Protein 0g

Bacon-Wrapped Figs

Prep Time: 15 min ▪ Start to Finish: 25 min ▪ 30 Figs

1 package (12 oz) fully cooked cottage or Canadian-style bacon
2 packages (8 oz each) dried whole Calimyrna figs, stems removed
30 pistachio nuts
30 small basil leaves

1 Heat oven to 425°F. Spray 15×10-inch pan with cooking spray. Cut each bacon slice in half.

2 Cut slit in each fig; stuff with nut. Place basil leaf on bacon strip; wrap around fig. Place seam side down in pan.

3 Bake 8 to 10 minutes or until bacon is brown. Serve warm with toothpicks.

1 Fig: Calories 55 (Calories from Fat 10); Total Fat 1g (Saturated Fat 0g); Cholesterol 5mg; Sodium 150mg; Total Carbohydrate 10g (Dietary Fiber 1g); Protein 3g

Do Ahead: Assemble appetizers 3 to 4 hours ahead of your party and refrigerate. You may need to add 1 to 2 minutes to the bake time.

Blue Cheese–Stuffed Grapes

Prep Time: 30 min ▪ Start to Finish: 30 min ▪ 48 Grapes

3/4 cup garlic-and-herbs spreadable cheese
1/4 cup crumbled blue cheese
1/4 cup chopped dried apricots
48 large red globe grapes
48 small walnut pieces
Fresh chopped chives, if desired

1 In medium bowl, mix spreadable cheese, blue cheese and apricots. Cut top off of each grape. Scoop out grape with melon baller, leaving enough for a firm shell. If necessary, cut small slice from bottom so grapes stand upright.

2 Carefully spoon about 1/2 teaspoon cheese mixture into each grape. Top each with walnut piece and chives.

1 Grape: Calories 20 (Calories from Fat 10); Total Fat 1g (Saturated Fat 1g); Cholesterol 5mg; Sodium 30mg; Total Carbohydrate 2g (Dietary Fiber 0g); Protein 1g

Red globe grapes are large grapes, about the size of a big marble. They are available in the fall and until mid-January.

Fruit Kabobs with Tropical Fruit Coulis

Prep Time: 40 min ▪ Start to Finish: 40 min ▪ 24 Appetizers

6 cups bite-size pieces assorted fresh fruit (pineapple, watermelon and
   cantaloupe)
1 cup green grapes
1 cup blueberries or red grapes
3 small star fruit, cut into 24 slices
2 large mangoes, peeled, seeds removed and cut into large pieces
24 skewers (6 inch)
¼ cup pineapple preserves

1 Thread 4 to 6 pieces of fruits (except mangoes) on each skewer. Place skewers on large serving platter; set aside.

2 In food processor, place mango pieces and pineapple preserves. Cover and process until smooth; pour into small serving bowl. Serve kabobs with mango coulis.

1 Serving: Calories 50 (Calories from Fat 0); Total Fat 0g (Saturated Fat 0g); Cholesterol 0mg; Sodium 0mg; Total Carbohydrate 12g (Dietary Fiber 1g); Protein 0g

Cut the watermelon with mini star-shaped cookie cutters. Place skewers in a clear glass vase. Or cut a fresh pineapple (including top) lengthwise in half. Place pineapple on serving platter, and insert skewers into pineapple. Serve coulis in a pretty cocktail glass.

Cheesy Apple Polenta Bites

Prep Time: 35 min ▪ Start to Finish: 12 hr 55 min ▪ 72 Appetizers

1 cup yellow cornmeal
1 cup cold water
2¾ cups boiling water
1 teaspoon salt
2 tablespoons grated onion
1 tablespoon chopped fresh or
    1 teaspoon dried sage leaves

1 cup shredded Cheddar
    cheese (4 oz)
1 small unpeeled apple
Juice of 1 medium lemon
    (2 to 3 tablespoons)

1 Line square baking dish, 8×8 inches, with foil, leaving 1 inch of foil overhanging at 2 opposite sides of pan; grease foil. In 2-quart saucepan, mix cornmeal and cold water. Stir in boiling water and salt. Cook about 5 minutes, stirring constantly, until mixture boils and thickens; reduce heat to low. Stir in onion, sage and ½ cup of the cheese. Cook uncovered 5 minutes, stirring occasionally; remove from heat.

2 Spread cornmeal mixture (polenta) in baking dish. Cover and refrigerate at least 12 hours until firm.

3 Heat oven to 400°F. Grease 15×10-inch pan. Remove polenta from baking dish, using foil edges to lift. Cut polenta into 6 rows by 6 rows to make 36 squares. Cut each square diagonally to make 2 triangles; place in pan. Bake uncovered about 15 minutes or until golden brown.

4 Cut apple into thin slices. Cut slices into fourths. Dip apple pieces into lemon juice to keep them from discoloring. Top each triangle with 1 apple piece. Sprinkle remaining ½ cup cheese over apple pieces. Bake about 5 minutes or until cheese is melted. Serve warm.

1 Appetizer: Calories 20 (Calories from Fat 10); Total Fat 1g (Saturated Fat 0g); Cholesterol 0mg; Sodium 40mg; Total Carbohydrate 2g (Dietary Fiber 0g); Protein 1g

Save time! Use purchased polenta, and eliminate the preparation step. Simply slice polenta, cut slices into fourths and bake as directed.

Cranberry–Chicken Salad Puffs

Smoked Salmon Puffs

Chiles Rellenos Puffs

Gorgonzola and Rosemary Cream Puffs

Fireside Popovers with Brie

Herb Popovers

Pepperoni Swirls

Ham and Gouda Pastry Puffs

Artichoke Triangles

Cheesy Onion and Tomato Puffs

Stilton Cheese Palmiers

Crab Bites

Pesto-Cheese Cups

Garden Phyllo Quiches

Basil Cheese Triangles

Chicken and Olive Pastries

Chili Cheese Empanaditas

4

savory pastries

Cranberry–Chicken Salad Puffs

Prep Time: 25 min ▪ Start to Finish: 1 hr ▪ 20 Puffs

- ½ cup water
- ¼ cup butter or margarine
- ½ cup all-purpose flour
- 2 eggs
- ½ pint deli chicken salad (1 cup)
- ¼ cup dried cranberries
- ¼ cup chopped pistachio nuts
- 1 teaspoon chopped fresh or ¼ teaspoon dried marjoram leaves

1 Heat oven to 400°F. Grease cookie sheet with shortening or spray with cooking spray. In 2½-quart saucepan, heat water and butter to rolling boil. Stir in flour; reduce heat to low. Stir vigorously over low heat about 1 minute or until mixture forms a ball; remove from heat.

2 Beat in eggs all at once with spoon; continue beating until smooth. Drop dough by heaping teaspoonfuls about 2 inches apart onto cookie sheet.

3 Bake about 18 minutes or until puffed and golden brown. Remove from oven; cut small slit with knife in side of each puff to allow steam to escape. Return to oven; bake 2 minutes longer. Cool away from draft about 10 minutes.

4 Meanwhile, in medium bowl, mix chicken salad, cranberries, nuts and marjoram.

5 Cut off top third of each puff; pull out any strands of dough. Spoon heaping teaspoonful of chicken salad into each puff.

1 Puff: Calories 75 (Calories from Fat 45); Total Fat 5g (Saturated Fat 2g); Cholesterol 30mg; Sodium 50mg; Total Carbohydrate 5g (Dietary Fiber 0g); Protein 3g

Do Ahead: Assemble these appetizers and refrigerate up to 2 hours before serving. Relax and enjoy the party!

Smoked Salmon Puffs

Prep Time: 15 min ▪ Start to Finish: 40 min ▪ 24 Puffs

1/2 cup Original Bisquick mix
1/2 cup milk
1/4 cup sour cream
1/2 teaspoon Worcestershire sauce
2 eggs
2/3 cup shredded Cheddar cheese
1/3 cup chopped smoked salmon
2 medium green onions, sliced (2 tablespoons)

1 Heat oven to 400°F. Spray 24 mini muffin cups with cooking spray.

2 In small bowl, beat Bisquick mix, milk, sour cream, Worcestershire sauce and eggs with fork until blended. Stir in remaining ingredients. Spoon about 1 tablespoon mixture into each muffin cup.

3 Bake 15 to 20 minutes or until golden. Cool 5 minutes. Loosen sides of puffs from pan; remove from pan. Serve warm.

1 Puffs: Calories 40 (Calories from Fat 20); Total Fat 2.5g (Saturated Fat 1g); Cholesterol 25mg; Sodium 80mg; Total Carbohydrate 2g (Dietary Fiber 0g); Protein 2g

Try other flavors! Havarti, Colby, mozzarella or Monterey Jack cheese would all be delicious.

Chiles Rellenos Puffs

Prep Time: 25 min ▪ Start to Finish: 1 hr ▪ 24 Puffs

1½ cups water
½ cup butter or margarine
1 cup all-purpose flour
½ cup cornmeal
1 teaspoon salt
6 eggs, beaten
¾ cup shredded Monterey Jack cheese (3 oz)
¾ cup shredded sharp Cheddar cheese (3 oz)
2 cans (4.5 oz each) chopped green chiles, drained

1 Heat oven to 400°F. Spray 24 regular-size muffin cups with cooking spray.* In 3-quart saucepan, heat water and butter over high heat to a full rolling boil. Remove from heat.

2 Stir in flour, cornmeal and salt until mixture forms a dough and all lumps have disappeared. Gradually stir in beaten eggs until well blended. Stir in both cheeses and the chiles. Divide dough evenly among muffin cups, filling each ¾ full.

3 Bake 25 to 29 minutes or until golden brown. Cool 2 minutes; remove from muffin cups. Serve warm.

1 Serving: Calories 110 (Calories from Fat 70); Total Fat 8g (Saturated Fat 4g); Cholesterol 70mg; Sodium 350mg; Total Carbohydrate 7g (Dietary Fiber 0g); Protein 4g

*If two 12-cup muffin pans are unavailable, spoon dough into pan; refrigerate remaining dough while baking first pan. Spoon refrigerated dough into pan; bake 28 to 35 minutes.

Gorgonzola and Rosemary Cream Puffs

Prep Time: 15 min ▪ Start to Finish: 45 min ▪ 25 Puffs

1/2 cup water
1/4 cup butter or margarine
1/2 cup all-purpose flour
1/4 teaspoon salt
1/4 teaspoon dried rosemary leaves, crushed
1/8 teaspoon coarsely ground pepper
2 eggs
1 cup crumbled Gorgonzola cheese (4 oz)
2 tablespoons chopped pistachio nuts

1 Heat oven to 425°F. Spray large cookie sheet with cooking spray.

2 In 3-quart saucepan, heat water and butter to boiling over medium heat. Add flour, salt, rosemary and pepper all at once; stir constantly 30 to 60 seconds or until mixture forms ball. Remove from heat. Add eggs, one at a time, beating with electric mixer on medium speed until mixture is well blended.

3 Drop mixture by heaping teaspoonfuls about 2 inches apart onto cookie sheet. Bake 15 to 20 minutes or until golden brown. Cool 5 minutes.

4 Gently press center of each puff with tip of spoon to make slight indentation. Sprinkle with cheese and nuts. Bake 2 to 4 minutes or until cheese is melted. Serve warm.

1 Puff: Calories 50 (Calories from Fat 35); Total Fat 4g (Saturated Fat 2g); Cholesterol 25mg; Sodium 105mg; Total Carbohydrate 2g (Dietary Fiber 0g); Protein 2g

Do Ahead: Prepare cream puff dough as directed except drop mixture by heaping teaspoonfuls onto cookie sheet covered with waxed paper. Freeze until firm. Place drops of dough in airtight container or resealable food-storage plastic bag. To bake, place frozen dough on cookie sheet and continue as directed.

Fireside Popovers with Brie

Prep Time: 10 min ▮ Start to Finish: 30 min ▮ 24 Popovers

2 eggs
1 cup all-purpose flour
1 cup milk
1 teaspoon sugar
1/2 teaspoon salt
1/2 lb Brie cheese, cut into 24 chunks

1 Heat oven to 450°F. Generously grease 24 small muffin cups (1 3/4 ×1 inch). In medium bowl, beat eggs slightly with fork or wire whisk. Beat in flour, milk, sugar and salt just until smooth (do not overbeat). Divide batter evenly among muffin cups. Bake 5 minutes.

2 Reduce oven temperature to 350°F. Bake about 10 minutes longer or until crusty and golden brown. Cut a small slit in top of each popover. Insert cheese chunk in each popover. Bake 5 minutes. Immediately remove from pans. Serve hot.

1 Appetizer: Calories 60 (Calories from Fat 25); Total Fat 3g (Saturated Fat 2g); Cholesterol 25mg; Sodium 140mg; Total Carbohydrate 5g (Dietary Fiber 0g); Protein 3g

Do Ahead: Bake popovers and cut the slit in top of each. Cool, wrap tightly and freeze. When ready to serve, insert cheese chunk in each frozen popover. Place in muffin cups. Heat in 350°F oven 8 to 10 minutes or until cheese is melted.

Herb Popovers

Prep Time: 5 min ▪ Start to Finish: 45 min ▪ 12 Popovers

2 cups all-purpose flour
2 cups fat-free (skim) milk
1 teaspoon dried basil leaves
½ teaspoon onion salt
2 eggs
4 egg whites

1 Heat oven to 450°F. Spray two 6-cup popover pans or twelve 6-ounce custard cups with cooking spray.

2 Place all ingredients in blender. Cover and blend on medium speed about 15 seconds, stopping blender to scrape sides if necessary, just until smooth.

3 Fill cups about ½ full. Bake 20 minutes.

4 Reduce oven temperature to 350°F. Bake 15 to 20 minutes longer or until deep golden brown. Immediately remove from cups. Serve hot.

1 Popover: Calories 100 (Calories from Fat 10); Total Fat 1g (Saturated Fat 0g); Cholesterol 35mg; Sodium 120mg; Total Carbohydrate 18g (Dietary Fiber 1g); Protein 6g

Perfect popovers are easy to achieve. Two tips: Don't underbake, and don't peek! Opening the oven door lets in cool air, which can cause the popovers to fall.

Pepperoni Swirls

Prep Time: 20 min ▪ Start to Finish: 3 hr 40 min ▪ 32 Swirls

1 sheet frozen puff pastry (from 17.3-oz package), thawed
3 tablespoons country-style Dijon mustard
4 oz pepperoni, chopped
1 cup shredded mozzarella cheese (4 oz)
2 teaspoons dried oregano leaves

1 On lightly floured surface, roll puff pastry into 16×14-inch rectangle. Spread mustard over all of pastry. Sprinkle pepperoni evenly over mustard. Sprinkle cheese and oregano over pepperoni.

2 Starting at 16-inch side, tightly roll up pastry; gently pinch edge into roll to seal. Wrap in plastic wrap and refrigerate 2 to 3 hours.

3 Heat oven to 425°F. Line cookie sheet with foil; lightly spray foil with cooking spray. Cut pastry into ½-inch slices. Place on cookie sheet.

4 Bake 15 to 20 minutes or until golden brown and slightly puffed. Serve warm.

1 Swirl: Calories 70 (Calories from Fat 45); Total Fat 5g (Saturated Fat 2g); Cholesterol 10mg; Sodium 140mg; Total Carbohydrate 3g (Dietary Fiber 0g); Protein 2g

A serrated knife works well for slicing these pastry swirl treats.

Ham and Gouda Pastry Puffs

Prep Time: 30 min ▪ Start to Finish: 55 min ▪ 36 Puffs

1¼ cups finely diced fully cooked ham
½ cup shredded Gouda cheese (2 oz)
¼ cup sun-dried tomatoes in oil, drained, chopped
2 tablespoons sour cream
4 medium green onions, chopped (¼ cup)
2 packages (17.3 oz each) frozen puff pastry sheets, thawed

1 Heat oven to 400°F. Mix all ingredients except pastry.

2 Cut pastry into circles with 2½- to 3-inch round cookie cutter or pastry wheel. Spoon about 1 rounded teaspoon ham mixture on center of each circle, brush edges with water. Fold each circle over filling, pressing edges to seal.

3 Place in ungreased 15×10-inch pan. Bake 18 to 22 minutes or until golden brown. Serve warm.

1 Puff: Calories 107 (Calories from Fat 110); Total Fat 12g (Saturated Fat 4g); Cholesterol 35mg; Sodium 160mg; Total Carbohydrate 13g (Dietary Fiber 0g); Protein 4g

Do Ahead: Prepare and bake puffs up to a day ahead of time. Cool completely, then cover and refrigerate no longer than 24 hours. Reheat in 400°F oven 6 to 8 minutes or until heated through. You can also freeze unbaked puffs. Place waxed paper or cooking parchment paper between layers of puffs. Cover lightly and freeze up to 1 week. Bake as directed.

Artichoke Triangles

Prep Time: 40 min ▪ Start to Finish: 1 hr 25 min ▪ 24 Appetizers

1 can (14 to 16 oz) artichoke hearts, well drained, chopped
1/2 cup mayonnaise or salad dressing
1/4 cup shredded Swiss cheese (1 oz)
1/4 cup freshly grated Parmesan cheese
1 clove garlic, finely chopped
1/8 teaspoon freshly cracked pepper
1 package (17.3 oz) frozen puff pastry sheets, thawed
2 tablespoons half-and-half

1 Heat oven to 400°F. Line large cookie sheet with foil or cooking parchment paper; lightly spray foil or paper with cooking spray. In medium bowl, mix all ingredients except pastry and half-and-half.

2 On lightly floured surface, roll 1 sheet of pastry into 12×9-inch rectangle, trimming edges if necessary. Cut into twelve 3-inch squares.

3 Place 1 tablespoon artichoke mixture on each square. Lightly brush edges with half-and-half. Fold pastry over filling to make triangles. Crimp edges with fork to seal. Place on cookie sheet. Repeat with remaining pastry and artichoke mixture. Brush tops of triangles with half-and-half. Refrigerate 20 minutes.

4 Bake 20 to 25 minutes or until golden brown. Serve warm.

1 Appetizer: Calories 170 (Calories from Fat 110); Total Fat 12g (Saturated Fat 4g); Cholesterol 30mg; Sodium 150mg; Total Carbohydrate 11g (Dietary Fiber 1g); Protein 3g

Cheesy Onion and Tomato Puffs

Prep Time: 25 min ▪ Start to Finish: 1 hr ▪ 36 Puffs

1 sheet frozen puff pastry (from 17.3-oz package), thawed
2 tablespoons butter or margarine
1 sweet onion, cut lengthwise into fourths and thinly sliced (2½ cups)
2 teaspoons packed brown sugar
¼ cup sun-dried tomatoes in oil and herbs, drained, finely chopped
1 round (4 oz) Camembert cheese, cut into ³/₄x³/₄x¹/₄-inch pieces

1 Heat oven to 400°F. Spray 2 cookie sheets with cooking spray. Unfold pastry on lightly floured surface. Roll into 12-inch square, trimming edges to make even. Cut into 6 rows by 6 rows to make 36 (2-inch) squares. Place on cookie sheets.

2 Bake 12 to 15 minutes, rearranging cookie sheets after 6 minutes, until puffed and golden brown. Remove from cookie sheets to wire rack. Cool until slightly warm.

3 Meanwhile, melt butter in 8-inch skillet over medium heat. Cook onion in butter 15 to 20 minutes, stirring occasionally, until tender. Stir in brown sugar. Cook and stir until onions are coated. Stir in tomatoes. Remove from heat; keep warm.

4 Place cooled pastry squares on same cookie sheets. Press cheese piece into center of each pastry square. Fill with about 1 teaspoon onion mixture. Bake about 1 minute or until cheese is melted.

1 Puff: Calories 50 (Calories from Fat 35); Total Fat 4g (Saturated Fat 2g); Cholesterol 10mg; Sodium 45mg; Total Carbohydrate 3g (Dietary Fiber 0g); Protein 1g

Do Ahead: The onion filling can be cooked, covered and refrigerated up to 24 hours ahead. Just before serving, assemble appetizers and bake as directed.

Stilton Cheese Palmiers

Prep Time: 10 min ▮ Start to Finish: 50 min ▮ 30 Palmiers

1 sheet frozen puff pastry (from 17.3-oz package), thawed
½ cup shredded or crumbled Stilton cheese (2 oz)
2 medium green onions, finely chopped (2 tablespoons)
1 tablespoon finely chopped red bell pepper

1 Place pastry on lightly floured surface. Cut lengthwise at perforations into 3 strips. Roll pastry slightly to smooth. Sprinkle each strip with cheese, onions and bell pepper.

2 Mark line lengthwise down center of each strip. Tightly roll each side toward center line, leaving ¼-inch space at center; press rolls slightly. Brush off any excess flour with fingers. Wrap tightly in plastic wrap. Refrigerate at least 30 minutes but no longer than 4 hours.

3 Heat oven to 400°F. Line cookie sheet with foil or cooking parchment paper. Cut rolls into ¼-inch slices. Place about 2 inches apart on cookie sheet. Bake about 10 minutes or until light golden brown. Serve warm or cool.

1 Palmier: Calories 55 (Calories from Fat 35); Total Fat 4g (Saturated Fat 2g); Cholesterol 10mg; Sodium 50mg; Total Carbohydrate 4g (Dietary Fiber 0g); Protein 1g

Sprinkle each strip with cheese, onions and bell pepper. Mark line lengthwise down center of each strip.

Tightly roll each side toward center line, leaving ¼-inch space at center; press roll slightly.

Crab Bites

Prep Time: 15 min ▪ Start to Finish: 40 min ▪ 45 Appetizers

3/4 cup mayonnaise or salad dressing
3/4 cup grated Parmesan cheese
1/2 teaspoon finely chopped garlic
8 medium green onions, finely chopped (1/2 cup)
1 can (14 oz) artichoke hearts, drained, diced
1 package (6 oz) ready-to-eat crabmeat, flaked
3 packages (2.1 oz each) frozen mini fillo dough shells (15 shells each), thawed

1 Heat oven to 375°F. Line cookie sheet with foil or cooking parchment paper.

2 In large bowl, mix all ingredients except fillo shells with spoon about 2 minutes or until well blended.

3 Place fillo shells on cookie sheet. Fill each shell with about 1 tablespoon crab mixture. Bake 20 to 25 minutes or until shells are puffed and golden brown. Serve warm.

1 Appetizer: Calories 50 (Calories from Fat 30); Total Fat 3.5g (Saturated Fat 0.5g); Cholesterol 5mg; Sodium 85mg; Total Carbohydrate 3g (Dietary Fiber 0g); Protein 2g

Add a little color! Garnish each crab bite with half of a cherry tomato.

Pesto-Cheese Cups

Prep Time: 20 min ▪ Start to Finish: 45 min ▪ 30 Cheese Cups

1 package (8 oz) cream cheese, softened
1 egg
½ cup shredded Swiss cheese (2 oz)
¼ cup basil pesto
2 medium green onions, chopped (2 tablespoons)
2 packages (2.1 oz each) frozen mini fillo dough shells (15 shells each)
⅓ cup shredded Swiss cheese (1½ oz)

1 Heat oven to 375°F. Line cookie sheet with foil or cooking parchment paper. In medium bowl, beat cream cheese and egg with wire whisk. Stir in ½ cup cheese, the pesto and onions.

2 Place fillo shells on cookie sheet. Fill each shell with slightly less than 1 tablespoon of the cheese mixture. Sprinkle each with ½ teaspoon of the ⅓ cup cheese.

3 Bake 20 to 25 minutes or until cups begin to turn golden brown and are puffed. Serve warm.

1 Cheese Cup: Calories 60 (Calories from Fat 45); Total Fat 5g (Saturated Fat 3g); Cholesterol 20mg; Sodium 65mg; Total Carbohydrate 3g (Dietary Fiber 0g); Protein 2g

Garden Phyllo Quiches

Prep Time: 30 min ▪ Start to Finish: 1 hr ▪ 8 Quiches

2 boxes (10 oz each) frozen chopped spinach, thawed, squeezed to drain
2 cups sliced fresh mushrooms (6 oz)
2 cups milk
1 teaspoon ground mustard
½ teaspoon salt
¼ teaspoon ground nutmeg
4 eggs
8 sheets frozen phyllo (filo) pastry (18x14 inch), thawed
4 teaspoons butter or margarine, melted
½ cup shredded mozzarella cheese (2 oz)

1 Heat oven to 350°F. Spray 10- or 12-inch skillet with cooking spray. In skillet, cook spinach and mushrooms over medium heat, stirring occasionally, until spinach is wilted and mushrooms are tender; remove from heat.

2 In medium bowl, mix milk, mustard, salt, nutmeg and eggs; set aside.

3 Spray eight 6-ounce custard cups with cooking spray. Place 1 phyllo sheet on flat surface; lightly brush with butter. Top with 3 phyllo sheets, brushing each with butter. Cut phyllo into fourths. Place 1 phyllo section in each custard cup. Repeat with remaining phyllo sheets. Trim overhanging edge of phyllo 1 inch from rim of cup.

4 Drain spinach mixture; divide evenly among cups. Pour about ⅓ cup egg mixture into each cup. Fold edges of phyllo toward center.

5 Arrange custard cups in 15×10-inch pan. Bake 15 to 20 minutes or until egg mixture is set. Sprinkle with cheese. Serve immediately.

1 Quiche: Calories 180 (Calories from Fat 65); Total Fat 7g (Saturated Fat 3g); Cholesterol 115mg; Sodium 380mg; Total Carbohydrate 20g (Dietary Fiber 2g); Protein 11g

First time with phyllo? Thaw phyllo sheets in the refrigerator overnight or according to package directions. Handle thawed phyllo sheets carefully; they tend to become brittle when handled too much.

Basil Cheese Triangles

Prep Time: 25 min ▮ Start to Finish: 40 min ▮ 72 Triangles

1 lb feta cheese
2 eggs, slightly beaten
1/4 cup finely chopped fresh or 1 tablespoon dried basil leaves
1/4 teaspoon white pepper
1 package (16 oz) frozen phyllo (filo) pastry sheets (18x14 inch), thawed
1/3 cup butter or margarine, melted

1 Heat oven to 400°F. Grease cookie sheet. In small bowl, crumble cheese; mash with fork. Stir in eggs, basil and white pepper until well mixed.

2 Cut phyllo sheets lengthwise into 2-inch strips. Cover with plastic wrap, then with damp towel to keep them from drying out. Place 1 level teaspoon cheese mixture on end of 1 strip. Fold strip over cheese mixture, end over end in triangular shape, to opposite end. Place on cookie sheet. Repeat with remaining strips and cheese mixture. Brush triangles lightly with butter.

3 Bake 12 to 15 minutes or until puffed and golden brown. Serve warm.

1 Triangle: Calories 45 (Calories from Fat 20); Total Fat 3g (Saturated Fat 1g); Cholesterol 10mg; Sodium 105mg; Total Carbohydrate 4g (Dietary Fiber 0g); Protein 2g

Do Ahead: Cover and refrigerate unbaked triangles up to 24 hours before baking; bake as directed. Or freeze tightly covered up to 2 months; increase bake time by 5 minutes.

Chicken and Olive Pastries

Prep Time: 25 min ▌ Start to Finish: 40 min ▌ 36 Appetizers

3 refrigerated pie crusts (from two 15-oz boxes)
1 package (9 oz) frozen diced cooked chicken (2 cups), thawed, chopped
3/4 cup shredded Monterey Jack cheese (3 oz)
1/2 cup sliced pimiento-stuffed green olives, drained
1/3 cup chopped drained pimientos
1/4 cup sour cream
4 medium green onions, finely chopped (1/4 cup)

1 Heat oven to 400°F. Cut pie crusts into circles with 2 1/2 - to 3-inch round cookie cutter or pastry wheel. Place 1 pastry circle in each of 36 small muffin cups (1 3/4 ×1 inch) pressing slightly.

2 Mix remaining ingredients except onions. Spoon about 1 tablespoon filling into each cup.

3 Bake 12 to 16 minutes or until pastry edges are golden brown. Sprinkle with onions.

1 Appetizer: Calories 95 (Calories from Fat 55); Total Fat 6g (Saturated Fat 2g); Cholesterol 10mg; Sodium 150mg; Total Carbohydrate 6g (Dietary Fiber 0g); Protein 4g

Do Ahead: Make the filling up to 2 days ahead of time; cover and refrigerate.

Chili Cheese Empanaditas

Prep Time: 30 min ▪ Start to Finish: 45 min ▪ 32 Empanaditas

1 box (15 oz) refrigerated pie crusts
3/4 cup finely shredded Mexican-style four-cheese blend (3 oz)
1/3 cup canned diced green chiles, drained
Yellow cornmeal
1 egg
1 tablespoon water
Chili powder
Sour cream, if desired
Taco sauce, if desired

1 Let pie crusts stand at room temperature 5 to 10 minutes. Heat oven to 400°F. In small bowl, mix cheese and chiles; set aside.

2 Unfold one pie crust, placing on surface lightly dusted with cornmeal. Roll to a 13-inch circle. Cut into sixteen 3-inch rounds, rerolling scraps as necessary. Repeat with remaining pie crust.

3 Spoon 1 teaspoon cheese mixture onto center of each pastry round. Moisten edges of pastry with water; fold pastry in half over filling. Seal edge with fork. Place on ungreased cookie sheet.

4 Lightly beat egg and water. Brush mixture on pastries; sprinkle with chili powder.

5 Bake 12 to 14 minutes or until golden brown. Serve warm with sour cream and taco sauce.

1 Empanadita: Calories 80 (Calories from Fat 45); Total Fat 5g (Saturated Fat 2g); Cholesterol 10mg; Sodium 140mg; Total Carbohydrate 7g (Dietary Fiber 0g); Protein 2g

You can freeze unbaked empanaditas up to 2 months. Place them on cookie sheets and freeze until firm. Transfer to a resealable plastic food-storage bag. Bake frozen empanaditas at 400°F for 12 to 17 minutes.

Caesar Beef Kabobs

Ginger-Orange Pork Kabobs

Antipasto Picks

Honey Mustard Chicken Tidbits

Ground Turkey Skewers

Slow Cooker Cranberry Barbecue Meatballs

Crab Cakes with Cilantro Salsa

Ginger-Scallop Bites

Baked Coconut Shrimp

Herbed Seafood Bruschetta

Basil- and Crabmeat-Topped Cucumbers

Mushroom-Olive Bruschetta

Sun-Dried Tomato and Bacon Bruschetta

Dill Havarti–Shrimp Appetizers

Gorgonzola and Caramelized Onion Appetizer

Beef Crostini with Pesto Mayonnaise

Barbecued Pork Crostini

Salmon Crostini

Winter Fruit Kabobs with Peach Glaze

Fruit-Shaped Cheese Balls

Fresh Basil–Wrapped Cheese Balls

5

holiday cocktail party

Caesar Beef Kabobs

Prep Time: 20 min ▪ Start to Finish: 1 hr 30 min ▪ 30 Kabobs

1 lb beef boneless sirloin steak (3/4 to 1 inch thick), cut into 1-inch pieces
1 medium red or green bell pepper, cut into 1-inch pieces
1 cup 1-inch pieces zucchini
1½ cups whole mushrooms
1½ cups cherry tomatoes
½ cup Caesar dressing
¼ teaspoon coarsely ground pepper
30 wooden skewers (6 to 8 inch)
Romaine lettuce leaves
Additional Caesar dressing, if desired
Chopped fresh chives, if desired

1 In large resealable food-storage plastic bag, place beef, bell pepper, zucchini, mushrooms and tomatoes. In 1-cup glass measuring cup, mix ½ cup dressing and the ground pepper; pour over beef and vegetables. Seal bag; turn to coat. Refrigerate at least 1 hour but no longer than 4 hours, turning bag occasionally. Meanwhile, soak skewers in water about 1 hour to prevent burning.

2 Set oven control to broil. Remove beef and vegetables from marinade; discard marinade. Remove skewers from water. Thread 1 or 2 pieces beef on each skewer and about 4 pieces assorted vegetables onto each skewer.

3 Spray broiler pan rack with cooking spray. Place kabobs on rack in broiler pan. Broil with tops 4 to 6 inches from medium heat 6 to 8 minutes for medium beef doneness, turning frequently.

4 Arrange lettuce on serving platter. Top with kabobs. Spoon additional dressing into small bowl for dipping; sprinkle with chives.

1 Kabob: Calories 35 (Calories from Fat 20); Total Fat 2g (Saturated Fat 0g); Cholesterol 10mg; Sodium 40mg; Total Carbohydrate 1g (Dietary Fiber 0g); Protein 3g

Ginger-Orange Pork Kabobs

Prep Time: 30 min ■ Start to Finish: 2 hr 40 min ■ 20 Kabobs

1 cup orange marmalade
⅓ cup dry sherry or orange juice
4 medium green onions, chopped (¼ cup)
1 tablespoon olive or vegetable oil
2 teaspoons prepared horseradish
½ teaspoon ground ginger
¼ teaspoon salt
1¾ lb pork tenderloin, cut into 1-inch cubes
20 wooden skewers (6 to 8 inch)

1 In small bowl, mix all ingredients except pork and skewers. Place pork cubes in resealable plastic food-storage bag. Pour half of the marmalade mixture over pork; seal bag. Refrigerate 2 to 3 hours, turning bag occasionally. Refrigerate remaining marmalade mixture to use as dipping sauce.

2 Meanwhile, soak skewers in water 30 minutes to prevent burning.

3 Set oven control to broil. Line 15×10-inch pan with foil or cooking parchment paper; lightly spray foil or paper with cooking spray. Remove pork from marinade. Discard any remaining marinade. Thread 2 pork cubes on end of each skewer. Place in pan.

4 Broil with tops 4 to 6 inches from heat 5 minutes. Turn skewers; broil about 5 minutes longer or just until pork is no longer pink in center. Meanwhile, in 1-quart saucepan, heat remaining marmalade mixture over medium heat, stirring occasionally, until bubbly; use as dipping sauce.

1 Appetizer: Calories 90 (Calories from Fat 20); Total Fat 2g (Saturated Fat 1g); Cholesterol 25mg; Sodium 45mg; Total Carbohydrate 8g (Dietary Fiber 0g); Protein 9g

Make sure to cut the pork into cubes of the same size so the meat will cook evenly.

Antipasto Picks

Prep Time: 30 min ▪ Start to Finish: 1 hr 30 min ▪ 14 Servings

⅓ cup extra-virgin olive oil
¼ cup red wine vinegar
1 teaspoon grated lemon peel
1 clove garlic, sliced
1 teaspoon Italian seasoning
½ teaspoon crushed red pepper flakes
½ lb mozzarella cheese, cut into ¾-inch cubes
1 jar (4.5 oz) whole mushrooms, drained
4 slices (3¼ oz) prosciutto (from deli)
8 thin slices hard salami, cut in half
28 bamboo skewers or toothpicks (4 inch)
½ cup medium pitted ripe olives, drained
1 jar (6 to 7 oz) marinated artichoke hearts, drained

1 In medium bowl, mix oil, vinegar, lemon peel, garlic, Italian seasoning and red pepper flakes. Stir in cheese and mushrooms. Cover; refrigerate at least 1 hour but no longer than 24 hours.

2 Cut prosciutto slices lengthwise into 1-inch strips, cut strips into about 3-inch pieces. Drain mushroom mixture.

3 Pleat prosciutto pieces and salami half-slices. Spear prosciutto or salami with skewers; add assortment of mushrooms, olives and/or artichokes to skewers. Add cheese cube to end of each skewer. (Each skewer should have 6 pieces.)

1 Serving (2 picks each): Calories 150 (Calories from Fat 100); Total Fat 12g (Saturated Fat 3.5g); Cholesterol 15mg; Sodium 360mg; Total Carbohydrate 3g (Dietary Fiber 1g); Protein 8g

Honey Mustard Chicken Tidbits

Prep Time: 15 min ▪ Start to Finish: 40 min ▪ 25 Servings

¼ cup honey mustard
3 tablespoons butter or margarine
1 teaspoon garlic salt
¾ cup garlic herb dry bread crumbs
1 lb chicken breast tenders (not breaded), cut into 1-inch pieces (about
    50 pieces)
Additional honey mustard, if desired

1 Heat oven to 400°F. Line cookie sheet with foil or cooking parchment paper; spray foil or paper with cooking spray.

2 In medium microwavable bowl, mix ¼ cup honey mustard, the butter and garlic salt. Microwave uncovered on High 45 to 60 seconds or until butter is melted.

3 Place bread crumbs in large resealable plastic food-storage bag. Add chicken pieces to mustard mixture; stir to coat. Shake chicken pieces in bag of bread crumbs until coated. Place on cookie sheet. Discard any remaining honey mustard and bread crumbs.

4 Bake 20 to 25 minutes or until no longer pink in center. Serve with additional honey mustard.

1 Serving (2 pieces): Calories 70 (Calories from Fat 35); Total Fat 4g (Saturated Fat 1g); Cholesterol 15mg; Sodium 130mg; Total Carbohydrate 3g (Dietary Fiber 0g); Protein 5g

Do Ahead: Coat the chicken pieces 2 to 3 hours before baking, then cover and refrigerate until it's time to bake them.

Ground Turkey Skewers

Prep Time: 40 min ▪ Start to Finish: 1 hr 5 min ▪ 24 Servings

24 wooden skewers (8 inch)
1 package (1.25 lb) ground turkey
¼ cup finely chopped pecans
¼ cup finely chopped onion
1 teaspoon ground cumin
2 cloves garlic, finely chopped
1 teaspoon chopped fresh thyme leaves
½ teaspoon salt
¼ teaspoon pepper
1¾ cups fruit chutney, warmed

1 Soak skewers in water 30 minutes to prevent burning.

2 Meanwhile, heat oven to 375°F. Line 15×10-inch pan with foil or cooking parchment paper; lightly spray foil or paper with cooking spray. In medium bowl, mix all ingredients except chutney. Shape 1 rounded tablespoon of the turkey mixture around top third of each skewer.

3 Place skewers in pan with turkey in center of pan and skewers to outside of pan.

4 Bake 20 to 25 minutes or until turkey is no longer pink in center. Just before serving, brush ¼ cup of the warmed chutney on turkey. Serve remaining chutney as dipping sauce.

1 Appetizer: Calories 70 (Calories from Fat 20); Total Fat 2g (Saturated Fat 0g); Cholesterol 15mg; Sodium 75mg; Total Carbohydrate 7g (Dietary Fiber 0g); Protein 5g

Do Ahead: Prepare skewers 4 to 5 hours ahead; cover and refrigerate until serving time, then bake as directed.

Slow Cooker Cranberry Barbecue Meatballs

Prep Time: 30 min ▪ Start to Finish: 3 hr 50 min ▪ 24 Servings

Meatballs

1 lb lean (at least 80%) ground beef
½ lb ground pork
1 medium onion, finely chopped (½ cup)
¼ cup unseasoned dry bread crumbs
½ teaspoon ground mustard
½ teaspoon seasoned salt
⅛ teaspoon pepper
1 egg

Sauce

1 cup barbecue sauce
½ cup cranberry-orange sauce (from 9.2-oz jar)
½ teaspoon ground mustard
½ teaspoon ground ginger
½ teaspoon salt
2 tablespoons chopped fresh parsley

1 Heat oven to 375°F. Spray 15×10-inch pan with cooking spray. In large bowl, mix all meatball ingredients. Shape into 1-inch meatballs (about 72). Place in pan. Bake 15 to 20 minutes or until no longer pink in center and juice is clear.

2 In 2- to 2½-quart slow cooker, mix all sauce ingredients except parsley until well blended. Add meatballs.

3 Cover and cook on Low heat setting 2 to 3 hours or until thoroughly heated. Stir in parsley. Serve meatballs with cocktail forks or toothpicks. Meatballs will hold on Low heat setting up to 2 hours; stir occasionally.

1 Serving (3 Meatballs): Calories 90 (Calories from Fat 35); Total Fat 4g (Saturated Fat 1.5g); Cholesterol 25mg; Sodium 210mg; Total Carbohydrate 8g (Dietary Fiber 0g); Protein 6g

These meatballs are great to bring to a gathering. Just place them in the slow cooker and plug it in when you get to your destination. You're ready to go without using the host's precious oven space!

Crab Cakes with Cilantro Salsa

Prep Time: 30 min ▪ Start to Finish: 40 min ▪ 16 Crab Cakes

Cilantro Salsa
1 can (15 oz) black beans, drained,
    rinsed
1 can (11 oz) vacuum-packed whole
    kernel corn, drained
1 large tomato, chopped (1 cup)
2 tablespoons lime juice
1 tablespoon olive or vegetable oil
1/2 cup chopped fresh cilantro
1/4 cup chopped red onion
2 teaspoons ground cumin
1 teaspoon sugar
1/4 teaspoon salt
Crab Cakes
3 cans (6 oz each) crabmeat,
    drained, flaked

1/2 cup finely chopped green bell
    pepper
1/2 cup Italian style dry bread
    crumbs
1/4 cup chopped cilantro
1 medium green onion, sliced
1/4 teaspoon salt
1/8 teaspoon ground red pepper
    (cayenne)
2 tablespoons mayonnaise or
    salad dressing
1 egg, beaten
2 tablespoons vegetable oil
2/3 cup Italian style dry bread
    crumbs

1 In medium bowl, stir together salsa ingredients; cover and refrigerate.

2 In medium bowl, stir together all crab cakes ingredients except 2 tablespoons vegetable oil and 2/3 cup bread crumbs. Shape mixture into 16 cakes, about 2 inches in diameter.

3 In 12-inch skillet, heat oil over medium heat. Coat crab cakes with 2/3 cup bread crumbs. Cook in oil 3 to 4 minutes on each side, turning once, until golden brown. Drain on paper towels. Serve with salsa.

1 Crab Cake: Calories 150 (Calories from Fat 50); Total Fat 5g (Saturated Fat 1g); Cholesterol 40mg; Sodium 330mg; Total Carbohydrate 16g (Dietary Fiber 2g); Protein 10g

Do Ahead: Make the salsa up to 24 hours before serving. Mix and shape the crab cakes up to 24 hours before cooking; store tightly covered in the refrigerator.

Ginger-Scallop Bites

Prep Time: 20 min ▪ Start to Finish: 20 min ▪ 24 Servings

Sauce
½ cup mayonnaise or salad dressing
2 tablespoons frozen orange juice concentrate, thawed
1 tablespoon finely chopped gingerroot
2 teaspoons grated orange peel
Scallops
2 tablespoons olive or vegetable oil
2 cloves garlic, finely chopped
1 tablespoon finely chopped gingerroot
1½ lb fresh bay scallops (about 24)
¼ teaspoon salt
¼ teaspoon coarsely ground pepper
2 tablespoons finely chopped fresh mint leaves
2 tablespoons finely chopped fresh parsley
1 tablespoon grated orange peel

1 In small bowl, mix all sauce ingredients until well blended. Cover and refrigerate until serving.

2 In 12-inch nonstick skillet, heat oil over medium heat. Cook garlic and 1 tablespoon gingerroot in oil 1 minute, stirring frequently. Add scallops; sprinkle with salt and pepper. Cook 2 to 4 minutes, stirring frequently, until scallops are white and opaque.

3 Transfer scallops to serving bowl using slotted spoon. Add mint, parsley and 1 tablespoon orange peel; toss to coat. Serve scallops with sauce.

1 Serving: Calories 65 (Calories from Fat 45); Total Fat 5g (Saturated Fat 1g); Cholesterol 5mg; Sodium 90mg; Total Carbohydrate 2g (Dietary Fiber 0g); Protein 3g

Do Ahead: Although the scallops are best if cooked just before serving, you can make the sauce mixture and store it in the refrigerator up to 24 hours ahead.

Baked Coconut Shrimp

Prep Time: 40 min ■ Start to Finish: 40 min ■ About 31 Servings

3/4 cup apricot preserves

2 tablespoons lime juice

1/2 teaspoon ground mustard

1/4 cup all-purpose flour

2 tablespoons packed brown sugar

1/4 teaspoon salt

Dash ground red pepper (cayenne)

1 egg

1 cup shredded coconut

1 lb uncooked deveined peeled medium (31 to 35 count) shrimp, thawed if frozen

2 tablespoons butter or margarine, melted

1 In 1-quart saucepan, mix apricot preserves, 1 tablespoon of the lime juice and the mustard. Cook over low heat, stirring occasionally, just until preserves are melted. Refrigerate while making shrimp.

2 Move oven rack to lowest position; heat oven to 425°F. Spray rack in broiler pan with cooking spray.

3 In shallow bowl, mix flour, brown sugar, salt and red pepper. In another shallow bowl, beat egg and remaining 1 tablespoon lime juice. In third shallow bowl, place coconut.

4 Coat each shrimp with flour mixture, then dip each side into egg mixture and coat well with coconut. Place on rack in broiler pan. Drizzle with butter.

5 Bake 7 to 8 minutes or until shrimp are pink and firm and coating is beginning to brown. Serve with preserves mixture.

1 Serving (1 shrimp and 1 teaspoon sauce): Calories 60 (Calories from Fat 20); Total Fat 2g (Saturated Fat 1.5g); Cholesterol 30mg; Sodium 60mg; Total Carbohydrate 8g (Dietary Fiber 0g); Protein 3g

Do Ahead: If you have time, coat the shrimp up to 2 hours ahead of time. Refrigerate covered, and bake just before serving.

Herbed Seafood Bruschetta

Prep Time: 15 min ▪ Start to Finish: 1 hr 25 min ▪ 36 Appetizers

1 can (6 oz) crabmeat, drained, cartilage removed and flaked
1 can (4 to 4½ oz) shrimp, drained, rinsed
2 medium plum (Roma) tomatoes, seeded, chopped (½ cup)
⅓ cup chopped sweet onion
1 tablespoon chopped fresh chives
1 tablespoon chopped fresh basil leaves
1 tablespoon chopped fresh mint leaves
1 tablespoon olive or vegetable oil
1 tablespoon lemon juice
1 teaspoon finely chopped garlic
1 loaf (1 lb) baguette French bread, cut into 36 slices
3 tablespoons olive or vegetable oil
Freshly ground pepper to taste

1 Mix all ingredients except baguette, 3 tablespoons oil and the pepper. Cover and refrigerate at least 1 hour to blend flavors but no longer than 24 hours.

2 Place baguette slices on ungreased cookie sheet. Brush with some of the 3 tablespoons oil; sprinkle with pepper. Broil with tops 4 to 6 inches from heat 1 to 3 minutes or until light golden brown; turn. Brush with remaining oil; sprinkle with pepper. Broil 1 to 3 minutes longer or until light golden brown.

3 Place seafood mixture in bowl. Arrange bowl and toasted baguette slices on serving platter.

1 Appetizer: Calories 60 (Calories from Fat 15); Total Fat 2g (Saturated Fat 0g); Cholesterol 10mg; Sodium 100mg; Total Carbohydrate 7g (Dietary Fiber 0g); Protein 3g

Do Ahead: Toast slices for bruschetta up to 1 day ahead. Cool and store in airtight container at room temperature.

Basil- and Crabmeat-Topped Cucumbers

Prep Time: 40 min ▪ Start to Finish: 40 min ▪ 36 Appetizers

1 medium English (seedless) cucumber
1 package (3 oz) cream cheese, softened
2 tablespoons mayonnaise or salad dressing
¼ cup chopped fresh basil leaves
2 tablespoons finely chopped red onion
2 teaspoons grated lemon peel
1 cup frozen crabmeat (from 6-oz package), thawed, drained and flaked
2 tablespoons capers, if desired
Small basil leaves or chopped fresh basil, if desired

1 Score cucumber lengthwise with tines of fork if desired. Cut into 36 (¼-inch) slices.

2 In small bowl, beat cream cheese with electric mixer on low speed until creamy. Beat in mayonnaise until well blended. Stir in chopped basil, onion, lemon peel and crabmeat.

3 Spread or pipe about 1 teaspoon crabmeat mixture on each cucumber slice. Sprinkle with capers. Garnish with basil leaves.

1 Appetizer: Calories 20 (Calories from Fat 20); Total Fat 2g (Saturated Fat 1g); Cholesterol 5mg; Sodium 35mg; Total Carbohydrate 0g (Dietary Fiber 0g); Protein 1g

If you can't find frozen crabmeat, use a 6-ounce can of crabmeat, well drained.

Mushroom-Olive Bruschetta

Prep Time: 20 min ▪ Start to Finish: 20 min ▪ 20 Appetizers

1 can (4 oz) mushrooms pieces and stems, drained
½ cup pitted kalamata or ripe olives
2 tablespoons capers, drained
1 clove garlic, sliced
2 tablespoons extra-virgin olive oil
1 tablespoon balsamic vinegar
10 slices French bread, toasted

1 Mix mushrooms, olives, capers and garlic in food processor bowl. Cover and process by using quick on-and-off motions until finely chopped. Add oil and vinegar; process just until mixed (do not overprocess).

2 Spread mushroom mixture on toasted bread. Cut slices in half.

1 Appetizer: Calories 105 (Calories from Fat 25); Total Fat 3g (Saturated Fat 1g); Cholesterol 0mg; Sodium 260mg; Total Carbohydrate 17g (Dietary Fiber 1g); Protein 3g

Add small curls of fresh Parmesan cheese and fresh marjoram leaves to the tops of these tangy treats.

Sun-Dried Tomato and Bacon Bruschetta

Prep Time: 35 min Start to Finish: 50 min 24 Servings

24 slices (½-inch-thick) baguette French bread (from 10-oz loaf)
½ cup julienne-cut sun-dried tomatoes packed in oil
½ cup chopped cooked bacon
¾ cup finely shredded fontina cheese (2 oz)
¼ cup finely chopped fresh parsley

1 Heat oven to 400°F. In ungreased 15×10-inch pan, place bread slices.

2 In strainer over small bowl, place tomatoes; press tomatoes to drain oil into bowl (2 to 3 tablespoons oil is needed). Brush oil on bread. Bake 5 to 7 minutes or until crisp.

3 Top bread slices with tomatoes, bacon and cheese. Bake about 5 minutes or until cheese is melted. Sprinkle with parsley. Serve warm.

1 Serving: Calories 70 (Calories from Fat 20); Total Fat 2.5g (Saturated Fat 1g); Cholesterol 0mg; Sodium 150mg; Total Carbohydrate 9g (Dietary Fiber 0g); Protein 3g

Dill Havarti–Shrimp Appetizers

Prep Time: 20 min ▪ Start to Finish: 20 min ▪ 24 Appetizers

24 pumpernickel cocktail bread slices
3 tablespoons Dijon mustard
1 tablespoon honey
6 slices (about 8 oz) dill Havarti cheese
24 cooked deveined peeled medium or large shrimp, thawed if frozen,
    tail shells removed
2 tablespoons finely chopped red bell pepper
2 tablespoons chopped fresh dill weed

1 Heat oven to 400°F. Place bread slices in ungreased 15×10-inch pan. Bake 4 to 6 minutes or until crisp.

2 In small bowl, mix mustard and honey; spread over bread slices. Cut cheese into 2-inch squares. Top each bread slice with cheese, shrimp and bell pepper. Sprinkle with dill weed.

3 Bake 3 to 5 minutes or until cheese is melted.

1 Appetizer: Calories 70 (Calories from Fat 35); Total Fat 4g (Saturated Fat 2g); Cholesterol 20mg; Sodium 180mg; Total Carbohydrate 4g (Dietary Fiber 0g); Protein 4g

If you can't find the dill-flavored Havarti, you can use regular Havarti or you might try Gouda for a flavor change.

Gorgonzola and Caramelized Onion Appetizer

Prep Time: 40 min ▮ Start to Finish: 40 min ▮ 16 Appetizers

1 tablespoon butter or margarine
3 medium onions, chopped (1½ cups)
2 teaspoons packed brown sugar
½ teaspoon balsamic or red wine vinegar
16 slices (½-inch-thick) baguette French bread (from 10-oz loaf)
3 tablespoons crumbled Gorgonzola cheese

1 In 7-inch skillet, melt butter over medium heat. Cook onions, brown sugar and vinegar in butter 20 to 25 minutes, stirring frequently, until onions are golden brown.

2 Set oven control to broil. Place baguette slices on ungreased cookie sheet. Broil with tops 4 to 6 inches from heat 1 to 2 minutes or until lightly toasted.

3 Spoon about 1 teaspoon caramelized onions evenly onto each baguette slice. Sprinkle with ½ teaspoon of the cheese. Broil about 1 minute or until cheese is melted.

1 Appetizer: Calories 100 (Calories from Fat 20); Total Fat 2g (Saturated Fat 1g); Cholesterol 5mg; Sodium 210mg; Total Carbohydrate 18g (Dietary Fiber 1g); Protein 3g

The onions can be cooked and refrigerated up to 48 hours ahead of time and reheated in a microwave oven. Assemble the appetizers just before broiling.

Beef Crostini with Pesto Mayonnaise

Prep Time: 20 min ▪ Start to Finish: 50 min ▪ 24 Appetizers

1¼ lb beef tenderloin
1 tablespoon olive or vegetable oil
½ teaspoon salt
½ teaspoon coarsely ground pepper
½ teaspoon crushed dried rosemary leaves
¼ cup basil pesto
¼ cup mayonnaise or salad dressing
24 diagonally cut slices (½-inch-thick) baguette French bread (from 10-oz loaf)
3 tablespoons olive or vegetable oil
24 small fresh basil leaves

1 Heat oven to 450°F. Place beef in ungreased shallow baking pan. Brush with 1 tablespoon oil; sprinkle all sides with salt, pepper and rosemary. Insert meat thermometer so tip is in thickest part of beef.

2 Bake uncovered 20 to 25 minutes or until thermometer reads at least 140°F. Cover beef with foil and let stand 10 to 15 minutes until thermometer reads 145°F.

3 While beef is baking, in small bowl, mix pesto and mayonnaise.

4 Reduce oven temperature to 400°F. Brush bread slices with 3 tablespoons oil. Place in ungreased 15×10-inch pan. Bake 6 to 8 minutes or until crisp.

5 Meanwhile, cut beef into thin slices. Top each bread slice with beef and 1 teaspoon pesto mayonnaise. Garnish with basil leaf. Arrange appetizers on serving platter.

1 Appetizer: Calories 105 (Calories from Fat 65); Total Fat 7g (Saturated Fat 2g); Cholesterol 15mg; Sodium 150mg; Total Carbohydrate 5g (Dietary Fiber 0g); Protein 6g

Do Ahead: Roast the beef up to 24 hours in advance. Wrap tightly and store in the refrigerator until serving.

Barbecued Pork Crostini

Prep Time: 20 min ▪ Start to Finish: 1 hr 35 min ▪ 32 Appetizers

Marinade
½ cup barbecue sauce
2 tablespoons packed brown sugar
2 tablespoons olive or vegetable oil
2 tablespoons white wine vinegar
2 tablespoons soy sauce
1 to 2 teaspoons red pepper sauce
2 cloves garlic finely chopped

Crostini
2 pork tenderloins (each about ¾ lb)
3 large red or yellow bell peppers, roasted and cut into strips
2 tablespoons olive or vegetable oil
1 tablespoon balsamic vinegar
Salt, to taste
2 cloves garlic, finely chopped
1 loaf (1 lb) French bread, cut into ½-inch slices

1 In resealable plastic food-storage bag, mix all marinade ingredients. Add pork, turning to coat. Seal bag and refrigerate, turning pork occasionally, at least 30 minutes but no longer than 12 hours.

2 Mix bell peppers, oil, vinegar, salt and garlic. Set aside.

3 Heat oven to 425°F. Remove pork from marinade; reserve marinade. Spray shallow roasting pan with cooking spray. Place pork in pan. Insert meat thermometer so tip is in thickest part of pork. Bake uncovered 25 to 30 minutes, brushing occasionally with marinade, until thermometer reads 155°F. Discard any remaining marinade. Cover pork and let stand about 15 minutes or until thermometer reads 160°F and pork is slightly pink in center. Cut pork into ¼-inch slices.

4 While pork is standing, place bread on ungreased cookie sheet. Bake 3 to 5 minutes or until toasted. Top bread with pork and bell peppers.

1 Appetizer: Calories 335 (Calories from Fat 80); Total Fat 9g (Saturated Fat 2g); Cholesterol 55mg; Sodium 750mg; Total Carbohydrate 40g (Dietary Fiber 2g); Protein 25g

Do Ahead: Make the bell pepper mixture and the marinade up to 2 days ahead of time. Cover and refrigerate.

Salmon Crostini

Prep Time: 15 min ■ Start to Finish: 20 min ■ 18 Appetizers

18 slices pumpernickel cocktail bread
1/3 cup onion-and-chive cream cheese spread (from 8-oz container)
18 slices salmon lox (6 oz)
18 very thin strips red or green bell pepper
18 sprigs fresh dill weed

1 Heat oven to 400°F. On ungreased cookie sheet, bake bread slices 4 to 5 minutes or until crisp.

2 Spread bread slices with cream cheese spread. Top with lox, bell pepper and dill weed sprigs.

1 Appetizer: Calories 40 (Calories from Fat 20); Total Fat 2g (Saturated Fat 1g); Cholesterol 4mg; Sodium 135mg; Total Carbohydrate 4g (Dietary Fiber 0g); Protein 2g

If you don't have pumpernickel cocktail bread, you can use French bread, cut into 1/4-inch-thick slices.

Winter Fruit Kabobs with Peach Glaze

Prep Time: 35 min ▮ Start to Finish: 35 min ▮ 16 Kabobs

16 skewers (8 inch)

6 cups bite-size pieces assorted fresh fruit (pineapple, pears, apples, kiwifruit, strawberries)

2 cups grapes

3/4 cup peach or apricot preserves

2 tablespoons butter or margarine

2 tablespoons orange-flavored liqueur or orange juice

1/4 teaspoon ground cinnamon

1 On each of sixteen 8-inch skewers, thread 4 to 6 pieces of fruit, including grapes. Place skewers on large cookie sheet; set aside.

2 In 1-quart saucepan, heat preserves, butter, liqueur and cinnamon over medium-high heat, stirring frequently, until butter is melted. Brush about 1/4 to 1/3 cup of preserves mixture over kabobs; reserve remaining preserves mixture.

3 Set oven control to broil. Broil kabobs with tops 4 to 6 inches from heat 2 minutes or until fruit is hot and glaze is bubbly. Serve warm or cold with remaining preserves mixture.

1 Kabob: Calories 110 (Calories from Fat 15); Total Fat 2g (Saturated Fat 1g); Cholesterol 0mg; Sodium 15mg; Total Carbohydrate 22g (Dietary Fiber 2g); Protein 0g

If you're using bamboo skewers, soak them in water at least 30 minutes before using to prevent burning.

Fruit-Shaped Cheese Balls

Prep Time: 30 min ▪ Start to Finish: 8 hr 30 min ▪ 12 servings each

4 oz blue cheese, crumbled (²/₃ cup)	⅓ cup grated Parmesan cheese
1 container (8 oz) sharp Cheddar cold-pack cheese food	4 drops yellow food color, if desired
2 packages (3 oz each) cream cheese, softened	1 stick cinnamon
	Lemon leaf
1 teaspoon Worcestershire sauce	Vegetable oil
Paprika	Brown paper
	Crackers, if desired

1 In medium bowl, mix blue cheese, cheese spread, cream cheese and Worcestershire sauce with fork until blended. Cover and refrigerate at least 8 hours until chilled.

2 Divide cheese mixture in half. Shape 1 half into a ball on waxed paper. Sprinkle another piece of waxed paper with paprika. Roll cheese ball in paprika, coating completely. Mold into apple shape (see photo on back cover).

3 Shape other half of cheese mixture into a ball on waxed paper. In covered container, shake Parmesan cheese and food color until cheese is evenly colored. Sprinkle another piece of waxed paper with cheese. Roll cheese ball in Parmesan cheese, coating completely. Mold into pear shape.

4 Make small depression in apple and pear for stem ends. Cut 2 small pieces from cinnamon stick. Insert cinnamon stick pieces for apple and pear stems. Insert lemon leaf in apple. Brush oil over small piece of brown paper; cut into leaf shape. Insert leaf in pear. Serve with crackers.

1 Serving: Calories 85 (Calories from Fat 65); Total Fat 7g (Saturated Fat 4g); Cholesterol 20mg; Sodium 300mg; Total Carbohydrate 1g (Dietary Fiber 0g); Protein 4g

Do Ahead: Store these artful cheese balls tightly covered in refrigerator up to 2 weeks or in freezer up to 4 weeks. If frozen, unwrap cheese ball about 1 hour before serving and let stand at room temperature to thaw. Or thaw loosely wrapped frozen cheese ball in refrigerator at least 8 hours.

Fresh Basil–Wrapped Cheese Balls

Prep Time: 15 min ▪ Start to Finish: 45 min ▪ 24 Appetizers

½ cup mascarpone cheese (4 oz)
½ cup crumbled Gorgonzola cheese (2 oz)
2 tablespoons grated Parmesan cheese
⅛ teaspoon pepper
24 fresh basil leaves, 2 to 2½ inches long

1 In small bowl, mix cheeses and pepper until blended. Cover and refrigerate about 30 minutes or until firm enough to shape into balls.

2 Shape 1½ teaspoons cheese mixture into a ball. Roll slightly to form an oval, about 1 inch long. Place on wide end of basil leaf; roll up. Roll leaf and cheese between fingers to form an oval. Repeat with remaining cheese mixture and basil leaves.

3 Serve immediately, or cover with plastic wrap and refrigerate until serving but no longer than 2 hours.

1 Appetizer: Calories 30 (Calories from Fat 25); Total Fat 3g (Saturated Fat 2g); Cholesterol 5mg; Sodium 55mg; Total Carbohydrate 0g (Dietary Fiber 0g); Protein 1g

If mascarpone isn't available, you can still make these tasty holiday treats. Use a 3-ounce package of cream cheese, softened.

Party Drinks

A party wouldn't be complete without beverages. Here are a few to accompany an assortment of small bites and satisfy a variety of tastes.

Italian Sodas

Prep Time: 5 min
Start to Finish: 5 min
30 Sodas

6 bottles (12.7 oz each) assorted
    flavored syrup for beverages
    (raspberry, peach, hazelnut)
10 to 12 bottles (1 liter each) club soda
Strawberries, peach slices, lime slices,
    lemon slices, raspberries

1. Chill syrups and club soda in refrigerator before serving.

2. Fill tall glass with ice. Add 2 to 3 tablespoons flavored syrup to each glass.

3. Fill glasses with club soda. Garnish with fruit.

1 Soda: Calories 185 (Calories from Fat 0); Total Fat 0g (Saturated Fat 0g); Cholesterol 0mg; Sodium 0mg; Total Carbohydrate 46g (Dietary Fiber 0g); Protein 0g

Try the favorite flavored syrups from your neighborhood coffee bars to make these refreshing drinks.

Chai Iced Tea

Prep Time: 5 min
Start to Finish: 1 hr 5 min
6 Servings

8 chai tea bags
4 cups hot water
1 tablespoon vanilla
1/4 to 1/2 cup packed brown sugar
1/2 cup orange-flavored cream soda
1/2 cup vanilla-flavored cream soda
1/2 cup milk
Cinnamon sticks, if desired

1. Chill glasses in freezer several hours before serving.

2. Steep tea bags in hot water 3 to 5 minutes. Remove bags. Stir vanilla and brown sugar into tea until sugar is dissolved. Stir in all remaining ingredients except cinnamon sticks. Refrigerate at least 1 to 2 hours to blend flavors.

3. Serve over ice. Garnish with cinnamon stick.

1 Serving: Calories 70 (Calories from Fat 0); Total Fat 0g (Saturated Fat 0g); Cholesterol 0mg; Sodium 25mg; Total Carbohydrate 15g (Dietary Fiber 0g); Protein 0g

Taste test the tea when you add the brown sugar. Depending on the brand of tea used, you might need more or less sugar.

Swedish Glögg

Prep Time: 10 min
Start to Finish: 1 hr
24 Servings (about 1/2 cup each)

10 whole cloves
7 cardamom pods, crushed
2 sticks cinnamon
1 piece (about 1/2 inch) gingerroot, if
    desired
2 cups water
10 whole blanched almonds, cut length-
    wise in half
1 3/4 cups raisins
1 cup pitted large prunes
1 orange, cut into fourths
2 bottles (750 ml each) dry red wine
1 3/4 cups brandy
1 1/3 cups vodka
1/3 cup sugar

1. Tie cloves, cardamom pods and seeds, cinnamon and gingerroot in cheesecloth bag. Heat spice bag, water, almonds, raisins, prunes and orange to boiling in 4-quart Dutch oven; reduce heat. Cover and simmer 45 minutes.

2. Remove spice bag, prunes and orange. (Reserve prunes for eating if desired.) Stir in remaining ingredients. Cover and heat over medium heat until mixture begins to bubble. Ladle almond half and a few raisins into each cup before filling with hot glögg.

1 Serving: Calories 155 (Calories from Fat 0); Total Fat 0g (Saturated Fat 0g); Cholesterol 0mg; Sodium 5mg; Total Carbohydrate 13g (Dietary Fiber 1g); Protein 1g

Mexican Coffee

Prep Time: 15 min
Start to Finish: 25 min
10 Servings (about 1 cup each)

12 cups water
1/2 cup packed brown sugar
4 tablespoons ground cinnamon
4 whole cloves
1 cup regular-grind coffee (dry)
1/2 cup chocolate-flavor syrup
1 teaspoon vanilla
Whipped cream, if desired

1. Heat water, brown sugar, cinnamon and cloves to boiling in Dutch oven, stirring to dissolve sugar. Stir in coffee; reduce heat to medium-low. Cover and simmer 5 minutes.

2. Stir in chocolate syrup and vanilla; remove from heat. Let stand 5 minutes for coffee grounds to settle. Strain coffee into coffee server or individual cups; discard grounds mixture. Serve with whipped cream.

1 Serving: Calories 90 (Calories from Fat 0); Total Fat 0g (Saturated Fat 0g); Cholesterol 0mg; Sodium 25mg; Total Carbohydrate 23g (Dietary Fiber 2g); Protein 1g

Pick up a shaker with coffee toppings, such as cocoa and cinnamon, from a coffee or gourmet food shop. Pass the shaker when serving mugs of the hot coffee so folks can sprinkle a topping or two over their whipped cream!

Peppermint Shortbread Bites

Pistachio Biscotti

Orange-Toffee-Almond Truffles

Luscious Chocolate Truffles

Brandy Crème Brûlée Bars

Grasshopper Bars

Luscious Lemon Squares

Creamy Caramel-Peach Parfaits

Milk Chocolate Fondue

Peanut Butter Fondue

Caramel-Coffee Fondue

Strawberry–Cream Puff Kabobs

White Chocolate–Dipped Strawberries

Tiny Lemon Gem Tarts

Mini Almond Cheesecakes

Mini Peanut Butter Cheesecakes

6
dessert morsels

Peppermint Shortbread Bites

Prep Time: 25 min ▪ Start to Finish: 2 hr ▪ 64 Cookies

1 cup butter, softened (do not use margarine)
½ cup powdered sugar
2 cups all-purpose flour
1 teaspoon peppermint extract
3 tablespoons finely crushed hard peppermint candies (about 6 candies)
1 tablespoon granulated sugar
3 oz vanilla-flavored candy coating (almond bark), melted

1 In large bowl, beat butter and powdered sugar with electric mixer on medium speed until fluffy. On low speed, beat in flour and peppermint extract.

2 On ungreased cookie sheet, pat dough into 6-inch square, about ¾ inch thick. Cover; refrigerate 30 minutes.

3 Heat oven to 325°F. On cookie sheet, cut dough into 8 rows by 8 rows, making 64 squares. With knife, separate rows by ¼ inch.

4 Bake 28 to 35 minutes or until set and edges are just starting to turn golden. Meanwhile, in small bowl, mix crushed candy and granulated sugar. In small resealable food-storage plastic bag, place melted candy coating. Seal bag; cut tiny hole in 1 bottom corner of bag.

5 Do not remove cookies from cookie sheet. Pipe candy coating over cookies. Before candy coating sets, sprinkle candy mixture over cookies. Place cookies on cooling racks. Cool completely, about 30 minutes.

1 Cookie: Calories 50 (Calories from Fat 30); Total Fat 3.5g (Saturated Fat 2g); Cholesterol 10mg; Sodium 20mg; Total Carbohydrate 5g (Dietary Fiber 0g); Protein 0g

These cookies will keep their shape better during baking if they're very cold when you put them in the oven.

Pistachio Biscotti

Prep Time: 25 min ▮ Start to Finish: 1 hr 55 min ▮ 36 Biscotti

$2/3$ cup sugar	$1/4$ teaspoon baking soda
$1/2$ cup vegetable oil	$1/4$ teaspoon salt
2 teaspoons vanilla	$1/2$ cup coarsely chopped pistachio
2 eggs	nuts
$2^{1}/2$ cups all-purpose flour	$1/2$ cup semisweet chocolate chips
1 teaspoon baking powder	1 teaspoon shortening

1 Heat oven to 350°F. In large bowl, beat sugar, oil, vanilla and eggs with spoon. Stir in flour, baking powder, baking soda, salt and nuts.

2 Place dough on lightly floured surface. Knead 15 times until smooth. On ungreased cookie sheet, shape half of dough at a time into 10×3-inch rectangle.

3 Bake 25 to 30 minutes or until toothpick inserted in center comes out clean. Cool on cookie sheet 15 minutes. Cut rectangle crosswise into $1/2$-inch slices. Place slices, cut sides down, on cookie sheet.

4 Bake about 15 minutes longer, turning once, until crisp and light brown. Immediately remove from cookie sheet to cooling rack. Cool completely, about 30 minutes.

5 In small microwavable bowl, microwave chocolate chips and shortening uncovered on High 30 to 60 seconds or until melted; stir until smooth. Drizzle chocolate over biscotti. Place on waxed paper until chocolate is set.

1 Serving: Calories 100 (Calories from Fat 45); Total Fat 5g (Saturated Fat 1g); Cholesterol 10mg; Sodium 45mg; Total Carbohydrate 12g (Dietary Fiber 0g); Protein 2g

That's Italian! Baked twice for a crunchy texture, biscotti are mildly sweet cookies meant to be dunked in coffee.

Orange-Toffee-Almond Truffles

Prep Time: 45 min ▮ Start to Finish: 3 hr 15 min ▮ About 30 Truffles

1⅓ cups semisweet chocolate chips (8 oz)
½ cup whipping cream
½ teaspoon grated orange peel
½ cup toffee bits
1 cup sliced almonds, chopped, toasted*

1 In large microwavable bowl, microwave chocolate chips uncovered on High about 1 minute or until softened; stir until smooth. (If not completely softened, continue microwaving in 15-second increments, stirring after each, until smooth.)

2 Stir whipping cream into chocolate until very smooth and glossy. Stir in orange peel and toffee bits. Cover and refrigerate about 2 hours or until firm.

3 In small bowl, place almonds. Shape chocolate mixture into 1-inch balls. Immediately roll balls in almonds, pressing to coat. Place on ungreased cookie sheet or in paper candy cups. Refrigerate about 30 minutes or until firm. Remove from refrigerator 20 minutes before serving.

1 Truffle: Calories 90 (Calories from Fat 60); Total Fat 6g (Saturated Fat 3g); Cholesterol 5mg; Sodium 20mg; Total Carbohydrate 8g (Dietary Fiber 0g); Protein 1g

*In shallow pan, bake almonds 6 to 10 minutes, stirring occasionally, until golden brown. Cool 15 minutes.

Feeling festive? At each place at the table, place a truffle wrapped in tulle and tied with a ribbon. Add a gift tag for a pretty and delicious place card.

Luscious Chocolate Truffles

Prep Time: 20 min ▪ Start to Finish: 1 hr 15 min ▪ About 15 Truffles

1 bag (12 oz) semisweet chocolate chips (2 cups)
2 tablespoons butter or margarine
¼ cup whipping cream
2 tablespoons liqueur (almond, cherry, coffee, hazelnut, Irish cream, orange,
   raspberry, etc.), if desired
1 tablespoon shortening
Finely chopped nuts, if desired
Finely chopped dried apricots, if desired
White chocolate baking bar, chopped, if desired

1 Line cookie sheet with foil or parchment paper. In 2-quart saucepan, melt 1 cup of the chocolate chips over low heat, stirring constantly; remove from heat. Stir in butter. Stir in whipping cream and liqueur. Refrigerate 10 to 15 minutes, stirring frequently, just until thick enough to hold a shape.

2 Drop mixture by teaspoonfuls onto cookie sheet. Shape into balls. (If mixture is too sticky, refrigerate until firm enough to shape.) Freeze 30 minutes.

3 Heat shortening and remaining 1 cup chocolate chips over low heat, stirring constantly, until chocolate is melted and mixture is smooth; remove from heat. Dip truffles, one at a time, into chocolate. Return to cookie sheet. Immediately sprinkle nuts and apricots over some of the truffles. Refrigerate 10 minutes or until coating is set.

4 In small saucepan, heat baking bar over low heat, stirring constantly, until melted. Drizzle over some of the truffles. Refrigerate just until set. Store in airtight container in refrigerator. Remove truffles from refrigerator about 30 minutes before serving; serve at room temperature.

1 Truffle: Calories 145 (Calories from Fat 90); Total Fat 10g (Saturated Fat 6g); Cholesterol 10mg; Sodium 15mg; Total Carbohydrate 14g (Dietary Fiber 1g); Protein 1g

Dessert Morsels **139**

Brandy Crème Brûlée Bars

Prep Time: 25 min ▮ Start to Finish: 2 hr 35 min ▮ 36 Bars

1 cup all-purpose flour
$^1/_2$ cup sugar
$^1/_2$ cup butter or margarine, softened
5 egg yolks
$^1/_4$ cup sugar
$1^1/_4$ cups whipping cream
1 tablespoon plus 1 teaspoon brandy or $1^1/_2$ teaspoons brandy extract
$^1/_3$ cup sugar

1 Heat oven to 350°F. In medium bowl, mix flour, $^1/_2$ cup sugar and the butter with spoon. Press on bottom and $^1/_2$ inch up sides of ungreased 9×9-inch pan. Bake 20 minutes.

2 Reduce oven temperature to 300°F. In small bowl, beat egg yolks and $^1/_4$ cup sugar with spoon until thick. Gradually stir in whipping cream and brandy. Pour over baked layer.

3 Bake 40 to 50 minutes or until custard is set and knife inserted in center comes out clean. Cool completely, about 1 hour. For bars, cut into 6 rows by 6 rows. Place bars on cookie sheet lined with waxed paper.

4 In heavy 1-quart saucepan, heat $^1/_3$ cup sugar over medium heat until sugar begins to melt. Stir until sugar is completely dissolved and caramel colored. Cool slightly until caramel has thickened slightly. Drizzle hot caramel over bars. (If caramel begins to harden, return to medium heat and stir until thin enough to drizzle.) After caramel on bars has hardened, cover and refrigerate bars up to 48 hours.

1 Serving: Calories 85 (Calories from Fat 55); Total Fat 6g (Saturated Fat 3g); Cholesterol 45mg; Sodium 20mg; Total Carbohydrate 9g (Dietary Fiber 0g); Protein 1g

Grasshopper Bars

Prep Time: 20 min ▌ Start to Finish: 4 hr 10 min ▌ 50 Bars

1 cup granulated sugar
1/2 cup butter or margarine, softened
1 teaspoon vanilla
2 eggs
2/3 cup all-purpose flour
1/2 cup unsweetened baking cocoa
1/2 teaspoon baking powder
1/2 teaspoon salt
3 cups powdered sugar
1/3 cup butter or margarine, softened
2 tablespoons green crème de menthe
2 tablespoons white crème de cacao
1 1/2 oz unsweetened baking chocolate

1 Heat oven to 350°F. Grease 8×8-inch pan. In medium bowl, beat granulated sugar, 1/2 cup butter, the vanilla and eggs with electric mixer on medium speed, or stir with spoon. Stir in flour, cocoa, baking powder and salt. Spread in pan.

2 Bake 25 to 30 minutes or until toothpick inserted in center comes out clean; cool 15 minutes. Mix remaining ingredients except chocolate; spread over brownies. Refrigerate 15 minutes.

3 In 1-quart saucepan, heat chocolate over low heat until melted; spread evenly over powdered sugar mixture. Refrigerate at least 3 hours. For bars, cut into 5 rows by 5 rows; cut each bar diagonally in half to form triangles.

1 Serving: Calories 95 (Calories from Fat 35); Total Fat 4g (Saturated Fat 2g); Cholesterol 15mg; Sodium 50mg; Total Carbohydrate 14g (Dietary Fiber 0g); Protein 1g

If you don't have the liqueurs on hand, use 1/4 cup milk plus 1/2 teaspoon peppermint extract instead.

Luscious Lemon Squares

Prep Time: 10 min ▪ Start to Finish: 1 hr ▪ 25 Squares

1 cup all-purpose flour
$^1/_2$ cup butter or margarine, softened
$^1/_4$ cup powdered sugar
1 cup granulated sugar
2 teaspoons grated lemon peel, if desired
2 tablespoons lemon juice
$^1/_2$ teaspoon baking powder
$^1/_4$ teaspoon salt
2 eggs
Powdered sugar

1 Heat oven to 350°F. In small bowl, mix flour, butter and $^1/_4$ cup powdered sugar with spoon. Press in bottom and $^1/_2$ inch up sides of ungreased 8-inch or 9-inch square pan. Bake 20 minutes.

2 Meanwhile, in medium bowl, beat granulated sugar, lemon peel, lemon juice, baking powder, salt and eggs with electric mixer on high speed about 3 minutes or until light and fluffy. Carefully pour over hot crust.

3 Bake 25 to 30 minutes or until no indentation remains when touched lightly in center. Cool; dust with powdered sugar. Cut into 5 rows by 5 rows.

1 Square: Calories 90 (Calories from Fat 35); Total Fat 4g (Saturated Fat 1g); Cholesterol 15mg; Sodium 80mg; Total Carbohydrate 13g (Dietary Fiber 0g); Protein 1g

Creamy Caramel-Peach Parfaits

Prep Time: 10 min ▪ Start to Finish: 10 min ▪ 6 Servings

2/3 cup caramel topping
1 container (8 oz) frozen whipped topping, thawed
5 soft molasses cookies, broken up, if desired
1 can (29 oz) sliced peaches, drained, cut into pieces

1 In small bowl, fold caramel topping into whipped topping.

2 Layer cookies, whipped topping mixture and peaches in 6 parfait or other tall glasses. Sprinkle with cookie crumbs. Serve immediately, or refrigerate until serving.

1 Serving: Calories 300 (Calories from Fat 90); Total Fat 10g (Saturated Fat 6g); Cholesterol 30mg; Sodium 230mg; Total Carbohydrate 53g (Dietary Fiber 3g); Protein 3g

Serving a bigger group? Make additional parfaits using fresh or canned pears and other soft fruits for variety.

Milk Chocolate Fondue

Prep Time: 15 min ▪ Start to Finish: 15 min ▪ 8 Servings

²/₃ cup half-and-half
1 bag (11.5 oz) milk chocolate chips (2 cups)
2 tablespoons liqueur (almond, cherry, coffee, hazelnut, Irish cream,
    orange raspberry), if desired
Dippers (pound cake cubes, strawberries, pineapple chunks, apple slices,
    marshmallows)

1 In 2-quart heavy saucepan, heat half-and-half and chocolate chips over low heat, stirring constantly, until chocolate is melted and mixture is smooth; remove from heat.

2 Stir in liqueur. Pour into fondue pot or chafing dish.

3 Spear dippers with fondue forks; dip into fondue. (If the fondue becomes too thick, stir in a small amount of half-and-half.)

1 Serving (¼ cup fondue and 6 dippers each): Calories 360 (Calories from Fat 180); Total Fat 20g (Saturated Fat 11g); Cholesterol 35mg; Sodium 55mg; Total Carbohydrate 42g (Dietary Fiber 3g); Protein 5g

Dark Chocolate Fondue: Substitute 1 bag (12 ounces) semisweet chocolate chips for the milk chocolate chips.

The possibilities are endless! Try angel food cake cubes, banana slices, brownie cubes, grapes, kiwifruit pieces, mandarin orange segments, maraschino cherries, miniature cream puffs.

Peanut Butter Fondue

Prep Time: 15 min ▪ Start to Finish: 15 min ▪ 6 Servings

2/3 cup packed brown sugar
1/4 cup half-and-half
1 tablespoon honey
3/4 cup creamy peanut butter
Dippers (apple slices, pound cake cubes, marshmallows)

1 In 2-quart saucepan, heat brown sugar, half-and-half and honey to boiling over medium heat, stirring occasionally. Stir in peanut butter until smooth. Pour into fondue pot or individual serving bowls.

2 Spear dippers with fondue forks; dip into fondue.

1 Serving (1/4 cup fondue and 6 dippers each): Calories 460 (Calories from Fat 200); Total Fat 22g (Saturated Fat 6g); Cholesterol 20mg; Sodium 180mg; Total Carbohydrate 57g (Dietary Fiber 3g); Protein 10g

Make this fondue even more fun! Use sugar-cone sundae cups for individual-size fondues, and consider these dippers:
• Purchased pound cake cut into cubes or seasonal shapes
• Animal crackers or graham cracker squares
• Marshmallows
• Strawberries, grapes, pineapple chunks, banana slices, apple slices and pear slices
• Small plain or chocolate-covered pretzel twists

Caramel-Coffee Fondue

Prep Time: 20 min ▪ Start to Finish: 20 min ▪ 8 Servings

1/4 cup water

1 tablespoon instant coffee crystals

1 can (14 oz) sweetened condensed milk (not evaporated)

1 bag (14 oz) caramels, unwrapped

1/2 cup coarsely chopped pecans

2 apples (1 Braeburn, 1 Granny Smith), cut into 1/2-inch slices

2 cups fresh pineapple chunks

1/2 package (16-oz size) pound cake, cut into 1-inch cubes (about 4 cups)

1 In 2-quart nonstick saucepan, heat water over high heat until hot. Dissolve coffee crystals in water.

2 Add condensed milk, caramels and pecans to coffee. Heat over medium-low heat, stirring frequently, until caramels are melted and mixture is hot. Pour mixture into fondue pot and keep warm.

3 Arrange apples, pineapple and cake on serving plate. Use skewers or fondue forks to dip into fondue.

1 Serving (1/4 cup dip, 4 apple slices, 3 pineapple chunks and 1/2 cup cake cubes each): Calories 590 (Calories from Fat 190); Total Fat 21g (Saturated Fat 10g); Cholesterol 55mg; Sodium 210mg; Total Carbohydrate 90g (Dietary Fiber 3g); Protein 9g

No fondue pot? Use a small slow cooker, uncovered, instead.

Strawberry–Cream Puff Kabobs

Prep Time: 15 min ▪ Start to Finish: 25 min ▪ 6 Kabobs

6 (10-inch) bamboo skewers
18 tiny frozen cream puffs (from 13.2-oz box), thawed
12 fresh medium strawberries (about 2/3 lb), stems removed if desired
2 tablespoons semisweet chocolate chips
1 tablespoon butter or margarine

1 Line cookie sheet with waxed paper. On each skewer, alternately thread 3 cream puffs and 2 strawberries.

2 In small resealable freezer plastic bag, place chocolate chips and butter. Seal bag. Microwave on High about 30 seconds or until melted. Squeeze bag to mix melted chips and butter.

3 Cut small tip from 1 bottom corner of bag. Drizzle chocolate mixture over kabobs. Place on cookie sheet. Refrigerate about 10 minutes or until set. Store in refrigerator.

1 Kabob: Calories 150 (Calories from Fat 90); Total Fat 10g (Saturated Fat 6g); Cholesterol 25mg; Sodium 20mg; Total Carbohydrate 13g (Dietary Fiber 1g); Protein 2g

Do Ahead: Kabobs can be covered with plastic wrap and refrigerated up to 24 hours before serving.

White Chocolate–Dipped Strawberries

Prep Time: 30 min ▮ Start to Finish: 1 hr ▮ 18 Strawberries

1 bag (12 oz) white baking chips (2 cups)
1 tablespoon shortening
18 large strawberries with leaves
½ cup semisweet chocolate chips
1 teaspoon shortening

1 Cover cookie sheet with waxed paper. In 2-quart saucepan, heat white baking chips and 1 tablespoon shortening over low heat, stirring constantly, until chips are melted.

2 For each strawberry, poke fork or toothpick into stem end, and dip three-fourths of the way into melted chips, leaving top of strawberry and leaves uncoated. Place on waxed paper–covered cookie sheet.

3 In 1-quart saucepan, heat semisweet chocolate chips and 1 teaspoon shortening over low heat, stirring constantly, until chocolate chips are melted. (Or place chocolate chips and shortening in small microwavable bowl. Microwave uncovered on Medium 1 minute; stir. Microwave 2 to 3 minutes longer, until mixture can be stirred smooth.)

4 Drizzle melted semisweet chocolate over dipped strawberries, using small spoon. Refrigerate uncovered about 30 minutes or until coating is set.

1 Strawberry: Calories 125 (Calories from Fat 70); Total Fat 8g (Saturated Fat 5g); Cholesterol 5mg; Sodium 20mg; Total Carbohydrate 15g (Dietary Fiber 1g); Protein 1g

Double Chocolate–Dipped Strawberries: Substitute 1 bag (12 ounces) semisweet or milk chocolate chips for the white baking chips.

Rinse strawberries just before you are ready to use them. If you wash and then refrigerate the strawberries ahead of time, they will turn mushy.

Tiny Lemon Gem Tarts

Prep Time: 1 hr 30 min ▪ Start to Finish: 2 hr 15 min ▪ 24 Tarts

½ cup butter or margarine,
softened
3 tablespoons granulated sugar
1 cup all-purpose flour
½ cup granulated sugar
1 tablespoon all-purpose flour

3 tablespoons fresh lemon juice
2 teaspoons grated lemon peel
¼ teaspoon baking powder
⅛ teaspoon salt
2 eggs
2 tablespoons powdered sugar

1 Heat oven to 350°F. Spray 24 mini muffin cups with cooking spray. In medium bowl, beat butter and 3 tablespoons granulated sugar with electric mixer on medium speed until well mixed. Beat in 1 cup flour until dough forms.

2 Shape dough into ¾-inch balls. Press 1 ball in bottom and up side of each muffin cup for crust. Bake 14 to 16 minutes or until edges begin to turn golden brown.

3 Meanwhile, in same bowl, beat remaining ingredients except powdered sugar on medium speed until well mixed.

4 Spoon 1 heaping tablespoon mixture evenly into each baked crust. Bake 10 to 12 minutes or until filling is light golden. Cool in pan 15 minutes; remove from pan to cooling racks. Cool completely, about 30 minutes.

5 Sift powdered sugar over tops of tarts. Store covered in refrigerator. If desired, sift additional powdered sugar over tarts just before serving.

1 Tart: Calories 90 (Calories from Fat 40); Total Fat 4.5g (Saturated Fat 2.5g); Cholesterol 30mg; Sodium 50mg; Total Carbohydrate 11g (Dietary Fiber 0g); Protein 1g

To freeze, arrange in a single layer on cookie sheets and freeze until firm. Then pop them in an airtight container and store in the freezer. To thaw, let stand at room temp for 30 minutes.

Mini Almond Cheesecakes

Prep Time: 15 min ▪ Start to Finish: 2 hr 55 min ▪ 12 Cheesecakes

12 vanilla wafers
1 package (8 oz) plus 1 package (3 oz) cream cheese, softened
1/4 cup sugar
2 tablespoons amaretto or 1/2 teaspoon almond extract
2 eggs
1/4 cup chopped almonds, toasted*

1 Heat oven to 350°F. Place paper baking cup in each of 12 regular-size muffin cups. Place 1 wafer, flat side down, in each cup.

2 In medium bowl, beat cream cheese and sugar with electric mixer on medium speed until fluffy. Beat in amaretto. Beat in eggs, one at a time. Divide cream cheese mixture evenly among muffin cups (about 3/4 full). Sprinkle with almonds.

3 Bake 20 to 25 minutes or until centers are firm. Immediately remove from pan to cooling rack. Cool 15 minutes. Cover and refrigerate at least 2 hours but no longer than 48 hours.

1 Cheesecake: Calories 160 (Calories from Fat 110); Total Fat 12g (Saturated Fat 6g); Cholesterol 65mg; Sodium 110mg; Total Carbohydrate 9g (Dietary Fiber 0g); Protein 4g

*In shallow pan, bake almonds 6 to 10 minutes, stirring occasionally, until golden brown. Cool 15 minutes.

Do Ahead: These wonderful make-ahead cheesecakes can be refrigerated up to 48 hours or tucked away in the freezer. To freeze, refrigerate cheesecakes 1 hour or until completely cooled, then place in a labeled airtight freezer container and freeze up to 2 months. About 2 hours before serving, remove container lid and place frozen cheesecakes in refrigerator to thaw.

Mini Peanut Butter Cheesecakes

Prep Time: 25 min ▪ Start to Finish: 2 hr 55 min ▪ 12 Cheesecakes

12 vanilla wafer cookies
1 package (8 oz) plus 1 package (3 oz) cream cheese, softened
¼ cup sugar
½ teaspoon vanilla
2 eggs
12 one-inch chocolate-covered peanut butter cup candies, unwrapped

1 Heat oven to 350°F. Place paper baking cup in each of 12 regular-size muffin cups. Place 1 wafer, flat side down, in each cup.

2 In medium bowl, beat cream cheese and sugar with electric mixer on high speed until fluffy. Beat in vanilla. Beat in eggs, one at a time. Divide cream cheese mixture evenly among muffin cups (about ¾ full). Press 1 candy into cheese mixture in each cup until even with top of cheese mixture.

3 Bake about 15 minutes or until set. Immediately remove from pan to cooling rack. Cool 15 minutes. Cover and refrigerate at least 2 hours but no longer than 5 days. Cover and refrigerate any remaining cheesecakes.

1 Cheesecake: Calories 140 (Calories from Fat 90); Total Fat 10g (Saturated Fat 5g); Cholesterol 60mg; Sodium 95mg; Total Carbohydrate 10g (Dietary Fiber 0g); Protein 3g

If you're not fond of peanut butter cup candies, you can use 1 tablespoon of miniature semisweet chocolate chips in place of each cup. Just press the chips gently into the cheese mixture with the bottom of a teaspoon.

Helpful Nutrition and Cooking Information

Recommended intake for a daily diet of 2,000 calories as set by the Food and Drug Administration

Total Fat	Less than 65g
Saturated Fat	Less than 20g
Cholesterol	Less than 300mg
Sodium	Less than 2,400mg
Total Carbohydrate	300g
Dietary Fiber	25g

Calculating Nutrition Information

- The first ingredient was used wherever a choice is given (such as $\frac{1}{3}$ cup sour cream or plain yogurt).

- The first ingredient amount was used wherever a range is given (such as 2 to 3 teaspoons).

- The first serving number was used wherever a range is given (such as 4 to 6 servings).

- "If desired" ingredients and recipe variations were not included (such as sprinkle with brown sugar, if desired).

- Only the amount of a marinade or frying oil that is absorbed by the food during preparation was calculated.

Ingredients Used in Recipe Testing and Nutrition Calculations

- The following ingredients, based on most commonly purchased ingredients, were used unless otherwise indicated: large eggs, 2% milk, 80%-lean ground beef, canned chicken broth and vegetable oil spread containing at least 65% fat when margarine was used.

- Solid vegetable shortening (not butter, margarine or nonstick cooking spray) was used to grease pans unless otherwise indicated.

Equipment Used in Recipe Testing

- Cookware and bakeware without nonstick coatings were used, unless otherwise indicated.

- No dark-colored, black or insulated bakeware was used.

- When a pan is specified, a metal pan was used; a baking dish or pie plate means ovenproof glass was used.

- An electric hand mixer was used for mixing when mixer speeds are specified.

Metric Conversion Guide

VOLUME

U.S. Units	Canadian Metric	Australian Metric
1/4 teaspoon	1 mL	1 ml
1/2 teaspoon	2 mL	2 ml
1 teaspoon	5 mL	5 ml
1 tablespoon	15 mL	20 ml
1/4 cup	50 mL	60 ml
1/3 cup	75 mL	80 ml
1/2 cup	125 mL	125 ml
2/3 cup	150 mL	170 ml
3/4 cup	175 mL	190 ml
1 cup	250 mL	250 ml
1 quart	1 liter	1 liter
1 1/2 quarts	1.5 liters	1.5 liters
2 quarts	2 liters	2 liters
2 1/2 quarts	2.5 liters	2.5 liters
3 quarts	3 liters	3 liters
4 quarts	4 liters	4 liters

WEIGHT

U.S. Units	Canadian Metric	Australian Metric
1 ounce	30 grams	30 grams
2 ounces	55 grams	60 grams
3 ounces	85 grams	90 grams
4 ounces (1/4 pound)	115 grams	125 grams
8 ounces (1/2 pound)	225 grams	225 grams
16 ounces (1 pound)	455 grams	500 grams
1 pound	455 grams	1/2 kilogram

MEASUREMENTS

Inches	Centimeters
1	2.5
2	5.0
3	7.5
4	10.0
5	12.5
6	15.0
7	17.5
8	20.5
9	23.0
10	25.5
11	28.0
12	30.5
13	33.0

TEMPERATURES

Fahrenheit	Celsius
32°	0°
212°	100°
250°	120°
275°	140°
300°	150°
325°	160°
350°	180°
375°	190°
400°	200°
425°	220°
450°	230°
475°	240°
500°	260°

NOTE: The recipes in this cookbook have not been developed or tested using metric measures. When converting recipes to metric, some variations in quality may be noted.

Index

Page numbers in italics indicate illustrations.

Whatever's on the menu, make it easy with *Betty Crocker*

Betty Crocker
chicken tonight
100 Recipes for the Way You Really Cook

Betty Crocker
comfort food
100 Recipes for the Way You Really Cook

Betty Crocker
just cupcakes
100 Recipes for the Way You Really Cook

Betty Crocker
outdoor food
100 Recipes for the Way You Really Cook

Betty Crocker
party food
100 Recipes for the Way You Really Cook

Betty Crocker
quick fixes
100 Recipes for the Way You Really Cook

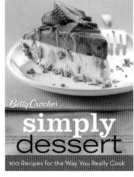

Betty Crocker
simply dessert
100 Recipes for the Way You Really Cook

Betty Crocker
small bites
100 Recipes for the Way You Really Cook